高等学校试用教材

建筑类专业英语
给水排水与环境保护

第一册

朱满才　王学玲　主编
胡继兰　孙晓梅
徐飞珍　吴晓光　编
项宏萍　　　　　主审

中国建筑工业出版社

《建筑类专业英语》编审委员会

总 主 编　徐铁城
总 主 审　杨匡汉
副总主编　（以姓氏笔划为序）
　　　　　王庆昌　乔梦铎　陆铁镛
　　　　　周保强　蔡英俊
编　　委　（以姓氏笔划为序）
　　　　　王久愉　王学玲　王翰邦　卢世伟
　　　　　孙　玮　李明章　朱满才　向小林
　　　　　向　阳　刘文瑛　余曼筠　孟祥杰
　　　　　张少凡　张文洁　张新建　赵三元
　　　　　阎岫峰　傅兴海　褚羞花　蔡慧俭
　　　　　濮宏魁
责任编辑　庞大中

前　言

　　经过几十年的探索，外语教学界许多人认为，工科院校外语教学的主要目的应该是："使学生能够利用外语这个工具，通过阅读去获取国外的与本专业有关的科技信息。"这既是我们建设有中国特色的社会主义的客观需要，也是在当前条件下工科院校外语教学可能完成的最高目标。事实上，教学大纲规定要使学生具有"较强"的阅读能力，而对其他方面的能力只有"一般"要求，就是这个意思。

　　大学本科的一、二年级，为外语教学的基础阶段。就英语来说，这个阶段要求掌握的词汇量为 2 400 个（去掉遗忘，平均每个课时 10 个单词）。加上中学阶段已经学会的 1 600 个单词，基础阶段结束时应掌握的词汇量为 4 000 个。仅仅掌握 4 000 个单词，能否看懂专业英文书刊呢？还不能。据统计，掌握 4 000 个单词，阅读一般的英文科技文献，生词量仍将有 6% 左右，即平均每百词有六个生词，还不能自由阅读。国外的外语教学专家认为，生词量在 3% 以下，才能不借助词典，自由阅读。此时可以通过上下文的联系，把不认识的生词猜出来，那么，怎么样才能把 6% 的生词量降低到 3% 以下呢？自然，需要让学生增加一部分词汇积累。问题是，要增加多少单词？要增加哪一些单词？统计资料表明，在每一个专业的科技文献中，本专业最常用的科技术语大约只有几百个，而且它们在文献中重复出现的频率很高。因此，在已经掌握 4 000 个单词的基础上，在专业阅读阶段中，有针对性地通过大量阅读，扩充大约 1 000 个与本专业密切有关的科技词汇，便可以逐步达到自由阅读本专业科技文献的目的。

　　早在八十年代中期，建设部系统院校外语教学研究会就组织编写了一套《土木建筑系列英语》，分八个专业，共 12 册。每个专业可选读其中的 3、4 册。那套教材在有关院校相应的专业使用多年，学生和任课教师反映良好。但是，根据当时的情况，那套教材定的起点较低（1 000 词起点），已不适合今天学生的情况。为此，在得到建设部人事教育劳动司的大力支持，并征得五个相关专业教学指导委员会同意之后，由建设部系统十几所院校一百余名外语教师和专业课教师按照统一的编写规划和要求，编写了这一套《建筑类专业英语》教材。

　　《建筑类专业英语》是根据国家教委颁发的《大学英语专业阅读阶段教学基本要求》编写的专业阅读教材，按照建筑类院校共同设置的五个较大的专业类别对口编写。五个专业类别为：建筑学与城市规划；建筑工程（即工业与民用建筑）；给水排水与环境保护；暖通、空调与燃气；建筑管理与财务会计。每个专业类别分别编写三册专业英语阅读教材，供该专业类别的学生在修完基础阶段英语后，在第五至第七学期专业阅读阶段使用，每学期一册。

　　上述五种专业英语教材语言规范，题材广泛，覆盖相关专业各自的主要内容：包括专业基础课、专业主干课及主要专业选修课，语言材料的难易度切合学生的实际水平；词汇以大学英语"通用词汇表"的4 000个单词为起点，每个专业类别的三册书将增加1 000～1 200个阅读本专业必需掌握的词汇。本教材重视语言技能训练，突出对阅读、翻译和写作能力的培养，以求达到《大学英语专业阅读阶段教学基本要求》所提出的教学目标："通过指导学生阅读有关专业的英语书刊和文献，使他们进一步提高阅读和翻译科技资料的能力，并能以英语为工具获取专业所需的信息。"

《建筑类专业英语》每册16个单元，每个单元一篇正课文（TEXT），两篇副课文（Reading Material A & B），每个单元平均2 000个词，三册48个单元，总共约有十万个词，相当于原版书三百多页。要培养较强的阅读能力，读十万个词的文献，是起码的要求。如果专业课教师在第六和第七学期，在学生通过学习本教材已经掌握了数百个专业科技词汇的基础上，配合专业课程的学习，再指定学生看一部分相应的专业英语科技文献，那将会既促进专业课的学习，又提高英语阅读能力，实为两得之举。

本教材不仅适用于在校学生，对于有志提高专业英语阅读能力的建筑行业广大在职工程技术人员，也是一套适用的自学教材。

建设部人事教育劳动司高教处和中国建设教育协会对这套教材的编写自始至终给予关注和支持；中国建筑工业出版社第五编辑室密切配合，参与从制定编写方案到审稿各个阶段的重要会议，给了我们很多帮助。在编写过程中，各参编学校相关专业的许多专家、教授对材料的选取、译文的审定都提出了许多宝贵意见。

本书为《建筑类专业英语》给水排水与环境保护专业第一册。本书在编写过程中，借鉴并采用了重庆建筑大学任慧清、吴瑞玲、张慰声、郭定寰、张显模、刘焕粤等同志所编写的《给水排水专业英语教材》第一册、第三册中的部分内容，同时本书承蒙刘绍根、汤利华、何开松等同志审阅了中文译文，谨此致谢。

《建筑类专业英语》是我们编写对口专业阅读教材的又一次尝试，由于编写者水平及经验有限，教材中不妥之处在所难免，敬请广大读者批评指正。

《建筑类专业英语》
编审委员会

Contents

UNIT ONE
    Text   History of Water Supply ··· 1
    Reading Material A   Major Water Pollutants (Ⅰ) ·· 6
    Reading Material B   Major Water Pollutants (Ⅱ) ·· 8

UNIT TWO
    Text   Water ··· 10
    Reading Material A   Importance of Water ·· 14
    Reading Material B   The Nature of Water ·· 15

UNIT THREE
    Text   Water Problems ··· 17
    Reading Material A   The Hydrologic Cycle ·· 21
    Reading Material B   The Hydrologic Cycle and Water Quality ···················· 22

UNIT FOUR
    Text   The Purification of Water ··· 24
    Reading Material A   Softening of Water ·· 28
    Reading Material B   Softening of Water ·· 29

UNIT FIVE
    Text   Basic Factors in Water Analysis ··· 31
    Reading Material A   Water Testing ··· 37
    Reading Material B   The General Physical-chemical Principle of Water ·············· 39

UNIT SIX
    Text   Water-supply Engineering ·· 41
    Reading Material A   Drainage, Sewerage and Sewage ································· 46
    Reading Material B   Water Supply ··· 48

UNIT SEVEN
    Text   Plumbing——Background and Status ·· 50
    Reading Material A   Basic Principles of Plumbing ······································· 54
    Reading Material B   Sources of Water ··· 55

UNIT EIGHT
    Text   Microbes as Chemical Machines ·· 58
    Reading Material A   Bacteria ·· 63
    Reading Material B   Water Pollution and Its Effect on Environment ·········· 65

UNIT NINE
    Text   Groundwater Formation and Its Movement ···································· 67
    Reading Material A   Sources of Water for Domestic Use ···························· 72

    Reading Material B   Multi-purpose Hydraulic Projects ……… 73

UNIT TEN
    Text   Open Channel Flow ……… 75
    Reading Material A   Dam ……… 79
    Reading Material B   Rock-fill Dams and Spillway ……… 80

UNIT ELEVEN
    Text   Environmental/Sanitary Engineering ……… 83
    Reading Material A   Sanitary Engineering ……… 87
    Reading Material B   Municipal Engineering ……… 88

UNIT TWELVE
    Text   Ecosystem ……… 91
    Reading Material A   Problems Due to Plankton-algae ……… 96
    Reading Material B   The Death of Microorganisms ……… 98

UNIT THIRTEEN
    Text   Factors Responsible for the Burgeoning Air Pollution Problem ……… 100
    Reading Material A   The "Killer Smog" ……… 105
    Reading Material B   Economic Loss from Air Pollution ……… 107

UNIT FOURTEEN
    Text   Solid Waste Disposal ……… 109
    Reading Material A   Where Do Pollution Come from? ……… 114
    Reading Material B   Industry Sludges ……… 116

UNIT FIFTEEN
    Text   Combating Water Pollution ……… 119
    Reading Material A   Ozone ……… 123
    Reading Material B   Acid Rain ……… 125

UNIT SIXTEEN
    Text   Paving the Way to Excellence in Water Supply System ……… 128
    Reading Material A   Control of Data Quality ……… 133
    Reading Material B   The Monitoring Approach of the Levels-of-service Framework ……… 135

Appendix Ⅰ   Vocabulary ……… 137
Appendix Ⅱ   Translation for Reference ……… 144
Appendix Ⅲ   Key to Exercises ……… 163

UNIT ONE

Text   History of Water Supply

[1]   Man's search for pure water began in prehistoric times. Much of his earliest activity is subject to speculation. Some individuals might have led water where they wanted it through trenches dug in the earth. Later, a hollow log was perhaps used as the first water pipe.

[2]   Thousands of years must have passed before our more recent ancestors learned to build cities and enjoy the convenience of water piped to the home and drains for water-carried wastes. ① Our earliest archeological records of central water supply and wastewater disposal date back about 5000 years, to Nippur of Sumeria. ② In the ruins of Nippur there is an arched drain with the stones set in full "voussoir" position, each stone being a wedge tapering downward into place. ③ Water was drawn from wells and cisterns. An extensive system of drainage conveyed the wastes from the palaces and residential districts of the city.

[3]   The earliest recorded knowledge of water treatment is in the Sanskrit medical lore and Egyptian Wall inscriptions. Sanskrit writings dating about 2000 B.C. tell how to purify foul water by boiling in copper vessels, exposing to sunlight, filtering through charcoal, and cooling in an earthen vessel.

[4]   The earliest known apparatus for clarifying liquids was pictured on Egyptian walls in the fifteenth and thirteenth centuries B.C. The first picture represents the siphoning of either water or settled wine. A second picture shows the use of wick siphons in an Egyptian kitchen.

[5]   The first engineering report on water supply and treatment was made in A.D. 98 by Sextus Julius Frontinus, water commissioner of Rome. He produced two books on the water supply of Rome. In these he described a settling reservoir at the head of one of the aqueducts. His writings were first translated into English by the noted hydraulic engineer Clemens Herschel in 1899.

[6]   In the eighth century A.D. an Arabian alchemist, Geber, wrote a rather specialized treatise on distillation that included various stills for water and other liquids.

[7]   The English philosopher Sir Francis Bacon wrote of his experiments on the purification of water by filtration, boiling, distillation and clarification by coagulation. This was published in 1627, one year after his death. Bacon also noted that clarifying water tends to improve health and increase the "pleasure of the eye".

[8]   The first known illustrated description of sand filters was published in 1685 by Luc Antonio Porzio, an Italian physician. He wrote a book on conserving the health of soldiers in camps, based on his experience in the Austro-Turkish War. This was probably the earliest published work on mass sanitation. He described and illustrated the use of sand filters and sedimentation. Porzio also stated that his filtration was the same as "by those who built the wells in the Palace of the Doges in Venice and in the palace of Cardinal Sachett, at Rome."④

[9]　　The oldest known archeological examples of water filtration are in Venice and the colonies she occupied. The ornate heads on the cisterns bear dates, but it is not known when the filters were placed. Venice, built on a series of islands, depended on catching and storing rainwater for its principal freshwater supply for over 1300 years. Cisterns were built and many were connected with sand filters. The rainwater ran off the house tops to the streets, where it was collected in stone-grated catch basins and then filtered through sand into cisterns.

[10]　　A comprehensive article on the water supply of Venice appeared in the Practical Mechanics Journal in 1863. The land area of Venice was 12.85 acres and the average yearly rainfall was 32 inches (in). Nearly all of this rainfall was collected in 177 public and 1900 private cisterns. These cisterns provided a daily average supply of about 4.2 gallons per capita per day (gpcd). This low consumption was due in part to the absence of sewers, the practice of washing clothes in the lagoon, and the universal drinking of wine. These cisterns continued to be the principal water supply of Venice until about the sixteenth century.

[11]　　Many experiments were conducted in the eighteenth and nineteenth centuries in England, France Germany, and Russia. Henry Darcy patented filters in France and England in 1856 and anticipated all aspects of the American rapid sand filter except coagulation. He appears to be the first to apply the laws of hydraulics to filter design. The first filter to supply water to a whole town was completed at Paisley, Scotland, in 1804, but this water was carted to consumers. In Glasgow, Scotland, in 1807 filtered water was piped to consumers.

[12]　　In the United States little attention was given to water treatment until after the Civil War. Turbidity was not as urgent a problem as in Europe. The first filters were of the slow sand type, similar to British design. About 1890 rapid sand filters were developed in the United States and coagulants were introduced to increase their efficiency. These filters soon evolved to our present rapid sand filters with slight modification.

New Words and Expressions

speculation [spekju'leiʃən]	n.	推测
trench [trentʃ]	n.	沟，渠
voussoir [vuːswɑː]	n.	（楔形）拱石，（拱）楔块
wedge [wedʒ]	n.	楔块，楔形物
taper * ['teipə]	v.	弄尖，（使）逐渐变细
cistern ['sistən]	n.	蓄水池，贮水器
drainage ['dreinidʒ]	n.	排水，排水设备；排出的水
Sanskrit ['sænskrit]	n.；a.	梵文（的）
lore [lɔː]	n.	（专门的）知识，（特殊的）学问
inscription [in'skripʃən]	n.	（铭）刻，碑文
foul * [faul]	a.	污浊的
earthen ['əːθən]	a.	土制的

siphon [ˌsaifən]	n.; v.	虹吸（管）；用虹吸管输送	
settle [ˌsetl]	v.	澄清，（使）沉淀	
wick [wik]	n.	灯芯，（吸）油绳	
aqueduct [ˌækwidʌkt]	n.	渡槽，沟渠	
hydraulic * [haiˌdrɔːlik]	a.	水力（学）的	
alchemist [ˌɔlkəmist]	n.	炼金术士	
treatise [ˌtriːtiz]	n.	（专题）论文	
distillation [distiˌleiʃən]	n.	蒸馏（法）	
still [stil]	n.	蒸馏（器）	
filtration * [filˈtreiʃən]	n.	过滤	
clarification [klærifiˈkeiʃən]	n.	澄清，净化	
coagulation [kəuægjuˈleiʃən]	n.	絮凝，混凝	
sanitation [sæniˈteiʃən]	n.	（环境）卫生	
sedimentation [sedimənˈteiʃən]	n.	沉淀，沉积	
ornate [ɔːˈneit]	a.	（装饰）华丽的	
grate [greit]	v.	装格栅于	
basin [ˈbeisn]	n.	水池，水槽	
catch basin		集水池，沉水池	
lagoon [ləˈguːn]	n.	污水池	
patent * [ˈpeitənt]	vt.; n.	为……取得专利；专利，专利品	
anticipate [ænˈtisipeit]	vt.	促进	
turbidity [təːˈbiditi]	n.	混浊（性），（混）浊度	
coagulant [kəuˈægjulənt]	n.	絮凝剂，凝洁剂	
modification * [mɔdifiˈkeiʃən]	n.	改变（进，良）	

Notes

①名词 the convenience 后有两个介词短语并列作后置定语，由 and 连接，第二个短语前省略了 of。

②Nippur of Sumeria 古巴比伦南部地区的一个古城。

③set in…position 为过去分词短语，修饰 the stones；each stone being…into place 为分词的独立结构；tapering…为现在分词短语，作 a wedge 的后置定语。

④关系代词 as 引导定语从句，和 the same 连用；as 从句有省略现象，完整的句子可为 as was used by those…。

Exercises

Reading Comprehension

Ⅰ. Say whether the following statements are True (T) or False (F) according to the text:
1. It is supposed that people in prehistoric times dug trenches to lead water where they wanted it. ( )
2. The central water supply and wastewater disposal systems found in the ruins of Nippur were probably the earliest built in human history. ( )
3. The pictures on Egyptian walls in the fifteenth and thirteenth centuries B. C. show the apparatus for filtering liquids. ( )
4. It is estimated that the use of siphons dates back about 1500 years. ( )
5. The famous hydraulic engineer Clemens Herschel produced two books on the water supply of Rome, in which he described a settling reservoir. ( )
6. In 1627, Sir Francis Bacon wrote of his experiments on the purification of water by distillation and illustrated various stills for water and other liquids. ( )
7. The earliest published work on mass sanitation written by Porzio described and illustrated the use of sand filters and sedimentation. ( )
8. The low consumption of water in Venice was due in part to the absence of sewers, the low levels of annual rainfall and the universal drinking of wine. ( )
9. Nenry Darcy's filters patented in 1856 were superior in all aspects except coagulation to those developed in America. ( )
10. Our present rapid sand filters are quite different from those developed in the late nineteenth century. ( )

Ⅱ. Identify main ideas for each paragraph by matching the following ideas with their appropriate paragraph numbers:
A. Frontinus made the first engineering report on water supply and treatment in A. D. 98. (9)
B. A comprehensive article on the water supply of Venice appeared in the Practical Mechanics Journal in 1863. (2)
C. The earliest records of central water supply and wastewater disposal date back about 5 000 years, to Nippur of Sumeria. (8)
D. Hency Darcy's filters patented in 1856 anticipated all aspects of the American rapid sand filters except coagulation. (5)
E. An Italian physician published the first known illustrated description of sand filters in 1685. (10)

Vocabulary

I. Fill in the blanks with the verbs given below, change the form if necessary:

| store | apply | show | evolve | produce |
| describe | date | provide | conserve | settle |

1. Water is a precious natural resource and one that should _____ but recycling is not just an environmental issue.
2. History _____ ample evidence of the potency of water-borne infection, with typhoid, cholera and dysentery as killer diseases.
3. In East Anglia a 16 Ha landfill _____ back to 1973 had seriously started to contaminate the underlying aquifer (含水层) and threaten local water supplies.
4. The wastewater treatment plant has proved highly effective in _____ water of the required specification and volume.
5. In the 1970s, the Chesapeake Bay _____ serious signs of illenss: algae blooms, low dissolved oxygen levels and loss of submerged aquatic vegetation.
6. Atlantic City _____ from a popular summer resort into a major east tourist and game center.
7. In agriculture throughout the developed world, it is normal management practice to _____ pesticides to protect crops against damage caused by pests, pathogens and weeds.
8. As common past practice, petroleum refinery waste _____ in open pits which now require remediation to meet current environmental regulations.
9. The consistency (稠度) of the sludge from the waste site can _____ as a viscous (粘稠的) semi-solid material, which varies from solid at some locations to a liquid at others.
10. One of the methods to remove solid wastes in water is sedimentation, in which wastes are allowed to _____ until they become solid or semisolid and can be removed.

II. Complete each of the following statements with one of the four choices given below:

1. Virtually all establishments where food is cooked, prepared or processed discharge some grease into the _____ system in the form of fats or cooking oils.
   A. voussoir   B. drainage   C. cistern   D. residential
2. Odour from sewerage, sewage treatment and trade effluents, can be _____ a great many substances.
   A. subject to   B. due to   C. based on   D. exposed to
3. Surface waters usually must be treated by _____ and chlorination to make them suitable for human consumption.
   A. filtration   B. sanitation   C. modification   D. purification
4. Rivers and streams have always been used to carry away domestic effluent——sewage——and before sewage systems and treatment works were constructed this prac-

tice made our rivers quite _____.
   A. urgent	B. ornate	C. universal	D. foul
5. Towards the end of the last century the relationship between polluted water _____ and disease became evident in UK and many other European countries.
   A. disposal	B. turbidity	C. consumption	D. coagulation

Reading Material A

Major Water Pollutants (I)

Water may be considered polluted because of an excess or burden of any gaseous, liquid, or solid constituent. The list of substances that may pollute water is almost endless, but the major pollutants are discussed here briefly.

Organic Wastes

Organic wastes are contributed by domestic sewage from both rural and urban areas and by industrial wastes of animal and plant origin. Although domestic sewage is the most widespread source of degradable organic wastes, industry contributes about an equal amount of such wastes. The greatest industrial generators of organic wastes are the food and pulp-and-paper industries, which have numerous plants, many of which discharge massive loads of organic wastes into waters.① One sugar beet processing plant during its brief seasonal operation may produce organic wastes equivalent to the sewage flow of a city of half a million people.

The breakdown of organic wastes by bacteria removes oxygen from the water, producing a serious problem. Since fish and aquatic life depend on dissolved oxygen, oxygen-demanding organic wastes damage the aquatic environment. When such wastes consume oxygen excessively, conditions of gross septic pollution result.

Living Agents

Living agents that can pollute water include bacteria, viruses, and other microorganisms that can cause disease. These organisms may enter water through domestic sewage or through certain kinds of industrial wastes, especially those associated with the tanning industry or animal slaughter. Although the bacteria causing typhoid and cholera are effectively controlled in most developed countries of the world, they still present a danger in many underdeveloped areas. Harder-to-destroy viruses that may cause intestinal or other infections pose a continuing water pollution problem.

Plant Nutrients

Plant nutrients-substances that stimulate the growth of plants- are also major polluters of water. The two principal water polluting elements in plant nutrients are nitrogen and phosphorus, but trace amounts of other elements are also present. These elements are usually present in small amounts in natural waters, but much larger amounts are contributed by sewage, certain industrial wastes, and drainage from fertilized lands and underground materials high in nitrates. Biological waste treatment processes do not remove plant nutrients from water. In fact, such treatment makes them more usable by plant life.

When plant nutrients spill over in large amounts into water, they act as fertilizers, stimulating the intensive and extensive growth of water plants, such as algae and water weed.② Such growth often causes unsightly conditions, interferes with water treatment processes, and creates unpleasant and disagreeable tastes and odors. When these plant growths die and decay, they not only produce a foul taste and odor but also cause secondary oxygen consumption, thus lowering the level of dissolved oxygen in the water. Such excessive development of plant life from surplus nutrients in surface streams, lakes, and ponds is known as eutrophication.③

Oil

Water is polluted by oil discharge from barges and ships or from the accidental or careless handling of crude oil in transport, development, and drilling operations. It is estimated that 1.5 million tons of oil are spilled into the ocean each year. Oil-polluted water results in great damage to aquatic life and other wildlife. Waterfowl alighting on oil sump areas or oil covered waters usually become so oil soaked that they are unable to fly. Oil destroys much of the aquatic life of oceans, including the food for fishes and shellfish. There is little information on the toxicological effects of oil on man or other warmblooded animals. Experience along the Santa Barbara coast of California indicates that severe oil spills also result in substantial immediate economic losses to the nearby communities.

Notes

①最大的工业有机废物的制造者是食品和纸浆造纸工业，这些工业有众多生产厂家，其中许多厂家都将大量的有机废物排入水体。
②当植物营养素大量流入水中时，它们便作为肥料而促使水生植物（如藻类和水草），密集而又大范围地生长。
③在地表的河流、湖泊和池塘中，由于过剩的营养素而造成的这种植物的过分生长被称为富营养化。

Reading Material B

Major Water Pollutants (II)

Synthetic Organic Chemicals

The steady output of new chemical compounds for a variety of purposes has produced new pollutants of increasing concern. New products are developed and old ones abandoned before their pollution significance can be determined.① In many chemical industries, for example, a majority of sales are of products unknown only two or three years earlier. Included in this group are detergents and many other household cleaning products, new synthetic pesticides, synthetic industrial chemicals of a wide variety, and wastes from the manufacture of these products.② In particular, pesticides, such as DDT, dieldrin, and chlordane, used to control insect pests in agricultural situations but eventually found in water, are of growing concern.③ The synthetic organic chemicals or their residues are often toxic to fish and other aquatic life as well as detrimental to man. Their stability and persistence in the water environment produce new and complex problems in conventional water and waste treatment.

Inorganic Chemical and Mineral Substances

Inorganic chemicals and minerals may also pollute water-interfering with stream purification, destroying fish and aquatic life, causing excessive hardness of water supply, having corrosive effects on machinery, and, in general, adding to the cost of water treatment. Included in this group are a vast array of metals, metal salts, acids, solid particulate matter, and many other synthetic chemical compounds and their by-products and wastes.

Mercury pollution has just recently been recognized as a very serious and widespread danger in many waterways. Abnormal amounts of mercury have been found in water and in fish and game birds in more than half of the states. Mercury, even in very small amounts, can cause very serious physiological effects and in some cases death. It, like the pesticides, travels along the food chain-that is, is passed from organism to organism, such as from minute aquatic microorganisms to fish to game birds or to man.④

Inorganic chemical pollutants are contributed to water through the wastes from mining and manufacturing processes, oil-field operation, agricultural practices, and natural sources. Irrigation, particularly in the western United States, leaches large amounts of mineral salts from the soil, adding substantially to the salt load of downstream water supplies. Natural salt and gypsum deposits in the southwest United States are particularly serious sources of pollution in that area, damaging or making unusable large quantities of ground, stream, and impounded water. Oil-field brines compound the salt problem in that region. Acids of a wide variety are discharged as waste by industry, particularly from abandoned workings and tailing of acid mine operations. Acid mine drainage is a major problem in the Ohio, Delaware, and Susquehanna rivers and in certain tributaries of the Mississippi River.

Cold Water

Cold water can also be a water pollutant, harming the production of some agricultural crops. Cold water released from the deep layers of storage reservoirs into surface streams of irrigation canals can, for example, have undesirable physiological effects on crops, retarding germination and reducing yields. This has happened in rice-growing areas in the Sacramento Valley of California. Cold water is also undesirable from the standpoint of recreational use.

Notes

①新、老产品在其污染性尚未能确定之前,便被开发利用或遭淘汰。
②在这一类污染物中,包括洗涤剂和许多其它家用洗涤产品,新的合成农药,品种繁多的合成化工产品及制造这些产品所产生的各类废物。
③特别是在农业环境中为防治虫害而使用的杀虫剂如滴滴涕,狄氏剂和氯丹,它们最终都出现在水体中,越来越令人担忧。
④象农药一样,汞会沿食物链转移,即由一个生物传给另一个生物,如由微小的水生微生物传给鱼、狩猎野禽或人。

UNIT TWO

Text   Water

[1]   In order to survive, all animals and plants must have an ample supply of water free from toxic materials and pathogenic microorganisms. As people congregate more and more in metropolitan areas, the problem of supplying an adequate quantity of pure water becomes greater and greater. One of the prime functions of the sanitary engineer is to ensure that there is always a safe supply of potable water. So well has the sanitary engineer done this job that it is possible to obtain pure, safe drinking water in some developed counties. Their citizens have become so accustomed to obtaining pure drinking water that they easily fall prey to contaminated water in many areas outside their countries.

Source of Water

[2]   All water comes in the form of precipitation. The heat of the sun evaporates water from the oceans, seas, rivers and lakes. The heat also evaporates water from the ground and from plants and animals. Water vapour is formed. This rises and forms clouds in the air. When the clouds come near a mountain, they are forced to rise. The higher they rise, the more they are cooled. This causes more and more water vapour to condense. In this way, the tiny drops of water in the clouds get bigger and bigger until they are heavy enough to fall to the Earth as rain.

[3]   As the water falls in the form of rain or snow or sleet or hail, it acts as a vacuum cleaner picking up all the dust and dirt in the air. Needless to say, the first water that falls picks up the greatest concentration of contaminants. After a short period of fall, the preciptation is relatively free of microorganisms.① When the water hits the ground, a portion of it runs off across the surface of the ground and a portion of it sinks into the ground.

Surface Water

[4]   The water running across the surface of the ground has been designated surface water. It picks up many substances as it flows back to the ocean, microorganisms, organic matter, and minerals.② Surface water collects in low areas forming lakes and ponds, and being rich in nutrients it becomes a perfect medium for the growth of all types of microorganisms. All forms of microbial life are found in surface waters. The types and numbers of microorganisms are a direct reflection of the condition in the water.

[5]   If the water is free of minerals, little, if any, biological life will be found. As more organic matter and minerals find their way into the surface water, bacteria, algae, and protozoa

grow. Fairly pure waters support few total numbers of microorganisms but have a relatively large number of different species. As more contaminants enter the water, the total number of microorganisms increases, while the number of species decreases. Waters high in inorganics show excellent algae growth, while waters polluted with organics show predominantly bacteria growths. Surface waters containing large numbers of microorganisms must be treated prior to use. Since "an ounce of prevention is worth a pound of cure," efforts are made to keep most surface reservoirs from becoming contaminated, thereby eliminating the need for extensive treatment.

Ground Water

[6]   The surface water which seeps into ground is designated ground water. As it travels through the surface layers of the earth, it picks up some minerals and a few organics in solution. The microorganisms and particulate matter find themselves being filtered out in the upper layers. Thus it is that most ground waters taken far below the earth's surface are free of microorganisms. These waters are usually relatively low in mineral and organic contaminants. Needless to say, ground waters are usually preferred as sources of drinking water to surface waters. ③

New Words and Expressions

toxic ['tɔksik]	a.	有毒的，中毒的
pathogenic [pæθə'dʒenik]	a.	致病的，病原的
microorganism [maikrəˈɔːgənizm]	n.	微生物
congregate ['kɔŋgrigeit]	v.	聚集
metropolitan [metrə'pɔlitən]	a.	大城市的
fall a prey to=suffer from		成为……的牺牲品
		深为……而苦恼
contaminate [kən'tæmineit]	vt.	污染，弄脏
precipitate* [pri'sipiteit]	v.	降水，沉降
precipitation* [prisipi'teiʃən]	n.	沉降物（如雨，雪等）
contaminant [kən'tæminənt]	n.	污染物质
hydrological [haidrə'lɔdʒikəl]	a.	水文学的
designate ['dezigneit]	vt.	表示，称为
nutrient ['njuːtriənt]	n.	养分，养科
medium ['miːdiəm]	n.	介质，培养基
microbial [mai'krəubiəl]	a.	微生物的，细菌的
algae ['ældʒiː]	n. (alga 的复数)	藻类，海藻
protozoa [prəutə'zəuə]	n.	原生动物

inorganics [inɔː'gæniks]	n.	无机物
predominantly* [pri'dɔminəntli]	ad.	显著地
seep [siːp]	vi.	渗入（into, in）
particulate [pə'tikjulit]	n.	粒子

Notes

①microorganisms, organic matter and minerals 是 substances 的同位语，中间插入以 as 引导的状语从句。

②ground waters are preferred to surface waters　地下水比地面水好。A is preferred to B：A 比 B 好（A 胜过 B）。

Exercises

Reading Comprehension

Ⅰ. Say whether the following statements are True (T) or False (F) according to the text.

1. While circulating in the ground, on the surface of the earth, water becomes polluted.　　　　　　　　　　　　　　　　　　　　　　　　　　　　　　( )

2. One of the main functions of the sanitary engineer is to ensure that there is always a safe supply of drinkable water.　　　　　　　　　　　　　　　　　　( )

3. Citizens from developed countries can drink pure, safe water from anywhere outside their countries.　　　　　　　　　　　　　　　　　　　　　　　　　　( )

4. After a short period of fall, the precipitation is absolutely free of microorganisms.　　　　　　　　　　　　　　　　　　　　　　　　　　　　　　　　( )

5. Lakes and ponds become perfect places for the growth of all types of microorganisms because there are plenty of nutrients in them.　　　　　　　　　　　　( )

6. Fresh waters have a relatively large number of different species, but few total numbers of microorganism.　　　　　　　　　　　　　　　　　　　　　　　　( )

7. When more contaminants find their way into the surface water, the total number of microorganism decreases, while the number of species increases.　　　　　( )

8. Algae growth is directly proportional to the total number of organics in water while bacteria growth is inversely proportional to it.　　　　　　　　　　　　　( )

9. When surface water seeps into ground, the microorganisms and particulate matter find themselves being filtered out in the upper layers.　　　　　　　　　( )

10. Ground waters are usually preferred as sources of drinking water, because they have relatively low minerals and organic contaminants.　　　　　　　　　( )

Ⅱ. Identify main ideas from each paragraph by matching the following ideas with their appropriate paragraph numbers.

A. Surface waters containing large numbers of microorganisms must (1)
   be treated prior to use.
B. All water comes in the form of precipitation. (6)
C. That people congregate more and more in metropolitan areas makes (4)
   the problem of supplying pure water greater and greater.
D. Ground waters are usually preferred as sources of drinking water. (2)
E. All forms of microbial life are found in surface waters. (5)

Vocabulary

I. Fill in the blanks with the words given below, change the forms if necessary:

| congregate | evaporate | condense | ensure | enter |
| designate | contain | eliminate | support | contaminate |

1. The water of the world _____ many of the chemical elements known to man.
2. Evaporation permits water to _____ the atmosphere, condense as clouds and eventually bring rain.
3. A portion of the water that enters the horizon of soil moisture may be either _____ or transpired.
4. The medicine will _____ you a good night's sleep.
5. The editors _____ the manuscript to half its original length.
6. The platform bridge over the railroad tracks _____ danger in crossing.
7. Water in which the presence of impurities is in such high quantity as to impair its uses may _____ as polluted water.
8. I _____ by him both materially and spiritually.
9. The city's water supply was in danger of _____ by surface drainage.
10. The clouds _____ in the sky. The higher they rise, the more they are cooled.

II. Complete each of the following statements with one of the four choices given below.

1. English is one of the world's _____ languages.
   A. preliminary   B. perceivable   C. predominant   D. prohibitive
2. The _____ of the heart is to send blood.
   A. action   B. response   C. function   D. foundation
3. Copper is a good _____ for the conduction of electricity.
   A. median   B. medium   C. mediocrity   D. medley
4. If the surface of reservoirs is polluted, _____ treatment of the water is needed.
   A. extensive   B. explosive   C. exclusive   D. excursive
5. The crystals gradually increase in size and finally drop from the cloud as _____
   A. snow   B. rain   C. sleet   D. thunder

13

Reading Material A

Importance of Water

Water is the best known and most abundant of all chemical compounds occurring in relatively pure form on the earth's surface. Oxygen, the most abundant chemical element, is present in combination with hydrogen to the extent of 89 percent in water. Water covers about three fourths of the earth's surface and permeates cracks of much solid land. The polar regions are overlaid with vast quantities of ice, and the atmosphere of the earth carries water vapor in quantities from 0.1 percent to 2 percent by weight. It has been estimated that the amount of water in the atmosphere above a square mile of land on a mild summer day is of the order of 50 000 tons. [1]

All life on earth depends upon water, the principal ingredient of living cells. The use of water by man, plants, and animals is universal. Without it there can be no life. Every living thing requires water. Man can go nearly two months without food, but can live only three or four days without water.

In our homes, whether in the city or in the country, water is essential for cleanliness and health. The average American family uses from 65 000 to 75 000 gallons of water per year for various household purposes.

Water can be considered as the principal raw material and the lowest cost raw material from which most of our farm produce is made. It is essential for the growth of crops and animals and is a very important factor in the production of milk and eggs. Animals and poultry, if constantly supplied with running water, will produce more meat, more milk, and more eggs per pound of food and per hour of labor. [2] For example, apples are 87% water. The tree on which they grow must have water many times the weight of the fruit. Potatoes are 75% water. To grow an acre of potatoes tons of water are required. Fish are 80% water. They not only consume water but must have large volumes of water in which to live. Milk is 88% water. To produce one quart of milk a cow requires from $3\frac{1}{2}$ to $5\frac{1}{2}$ quarts of water. Beef is 77% water. To produce a pound of beef an animal must drink many times that much water. If there is a shortage of water, there will be a decline in farm production, just as a shortage of steel will cause a decrease in the production of automobiles.

In addition to the direct use of water in our homes and on the farm, there are many indirect ways in which water affects our lives. In manufacturing, generation of electric power, transportation, recreation, and in many other ways water plays a very important role.

Our use of water is increasing rapidly with our growing population. Already there are acute shortages of both surface and underground waters in many localities. Careless pollution and contamination of our streams, lakes, and underground sources has greatly impaired the quality of the water which we do have available. It is therefore of utmost importance for our future that good conservation and sanitary measures be practiced by everyone. ②

Notes

①据估计，温暖的夏日里，每平方英里土地上大气中的水含量约为 5 万吨。
②如果一直用流水饲养牲畜和家禽，那么所耗的每磅饲料和每个工时就能生产更多的肉、奶、蛋。
③因此，人人都需对水采取保护措施和卫生措施，这一点对我们的未来是极其重要的。

Reading Material B

The Nature of Water

Physical Properties

In comparison with most other substances, water has most unusual physical properties. It occurs and is in common use in all three states——solid, liquid and vapor. Although of low molecular weight (approximately 18), it has a high boiling point. Neon, with very nearly the same molecular weight (slightly above 20), boils at -245.9℃. Water exists as a liquid through a long range of temperatures. At 374.0℃ and at a pressure of 217.7 atmospheres, it can no longer remain a liquid, these being respectively its critical temperature and critical pressure. The density of liquid water is unusual in that it increases slightly from its freezing point to 4℃ after which the density decreases with temperature rise, as in other liquids①. Its boiling point is quite dependent on atmospheric perssuer, being 100℃ at 760 millimeters (general pressure range at sea level) and about 84℃ at about 420 mm. The effect of pressure on the freezing point is not so marked. At 1 atmosphere (760 mm), water, water vapor, and ice are at equilibrium at 0℃. An increase of pressure to 100 atmospheres lowers the melting point of ice only to -1℃. At 2 000 atmospheres ice melts at -35℃, but at 5 000 atmospheres the solid state exists at nearly twice the temperature of boiling water. There are six different forms of ice, depending on pressure, but none are stable at ordinary atmospheric pressure except the one common form. ②

The change of volume when water freezes is its most striking property, there being an increase in volume of around 11 percent. Expansion involved as ice forms produces powerful forces, manifest in damage to plumbing, cracking of pavements, and weathering of rocks. ③ In bodies if water ice rises as it freezes and insulates the water below it, so that continued cold is required before ice forms to excessive depths.

Other physical properties of water, particularly its thermal properties, make it industrially useful. The standard thermal units, the calorie and the British thermal unit (Btu.) are based on water, the former being the quantity of heat required to raise one gram of water at its maximum density through one centigrade degree, and the latter, one avoirdupois pound of water through one Fahrenheit degree. (The unit, kilocalorie, or 1,000 calories, is more common.) Approximately 80 calories must be removed from one gram of water at 0℃ to convert it to ice, and about 540 calories are required to convert water at 100℃ to steam. The latter figure is important when condensing steam is employed in domestic and industrial heating systems.

Chemistry

Since the physical properties of water are dependent upon its chemical structure and composition, some of these properties will be covered in the following discussion of the chemistry of water.

The ancient philosophers included water among the four elements, the other three being earth, air, and fire. The term "element" had a much different meaning at that time, and water represented the properties of cold and fluidity. After the discovery of oxygen and hydrogen, Henry Cavendish (sometime before 1783) caused the two to combine by means of an electric spark, and thus established the composition of water, the reaction being $2H_2+O_2=2H_2O$. It was also observed that two volumes of hydrogen exactly combined with one volume of oxygen. The composition of water was also determined by the action of hydrogen on heated copper oxide, water and metallic copper being formed. The reaction in this case is $CuO+H_2=Cu+H_2O$.

Notes

① 液态水的密度独特性在于：从冰点到4℃之间，密度稍稍增大；4℃以上时密度随温度上升而减少，这一点与其它液体一样。
② 根据压力的不同，冰有六种形式。但除了普通冰之外，没有一种冰在常压下呈稳定状态。
③ 结冰引起的膨胀会产生强大的力，表现为毁坏管道，胀裂路面和风化岩石。

UNIT THREE

Text   Water Problems

[1]   Some rain water which falls on the Earth is evaporated by the sun's heat. Some of it sinks into the ground. It may be used up by thirsty plants. It may reach a well or a spring. Most of the water goes back to the rivers, seas and oceans. This process then starts all over again. The process is called the Water Cycle.

[2]   The environment in which modern man lives is the result of a complex process which began with the origins of life on earth and, but for the presence of water, could not have developed as we now know it. All living things require water to survive, from desert plants that germinate and flower briefly after infrequent rain, to man himself whose dependence on water to drink and to produce food is fundamental. ① When we consider man's needs in the environment he has created for himself, the problems of water quality assume alarming proportions.

[3]   Primitive man realized very early in his development that water was essential to his existence; he needed water to drink, the plants and animals he required for food flourished only where there was an adequate water supply. ②He found that water could be useful as a defence against his enemies , that it was a useful source of power, and that too much could lead to chaos and destruction. In modern times, the horrors of drought in Ethiopia and the results of severe flooding in Bangladesh are vivid illustrations of the important place of water in the environment.

[4]   For thousands of years man has been aware of his need of water in the right quantity. But, as his technology developed, as urbanization began, so pollution commenced, and slowly the need was realized for water of adequate quality. It is a sad fact that in the industrialized societies of the world, greed and technology have outstripped science. This has resulted in many rivers and water courses becoming heavily polluted by urban and industrial effluents, and the population of towns and villages dependent on a river for water becoming exposed to epidemics of water-borne diseases and to excessive amounts of trace metals,③ because of the lack of knowledge and equipment of monitor and control the quality of water in the environment.

[5]   This lack of knowledge is best illustrated by the fact that the science of bacteriology was not fully appreciated until the mid-nineteenth century, and for several decades after this many water supplies continued to be drawn from rivers downstream of effluent discharges which received little or no treatment; annual rounds of typhoid and cholera were a regular feature of life and death. Control of water quality by careful selection of sources and treatment processes has virtually eradicated water-borne epidemics in the developed countries. But there still remains a problem in the third world.

[6]   The lack of equipment is shown in the current concern over lead in the environment. It is only in the last 20-30 years that reliable equipment has been readily available to measure ac-

curately lead (and other elements) in very low quantities and, more important, to assess the effect of lead on the human body.

[7]   Today the human race appears to have reached the point at which it has realized many of its mistakes in the misuse of water, and is laying down standards, recommendations and guidelines, to control water quality at various stages in the water cycle in an attempt to reverse a trend which, in developed countries, had almost reached disaster level.

[8]   The fraction of the water cycle we are concerned about here is the 3% existing as fresh water, and it is this 3% that is generally available to man for purposes of health, food (agriculture and freshwater fisheries), industry and leisure. Because of this, measuring, monitoring and controlling quality in this portion of the cycle is important to all societies.

[9]   When considering how to do this in detail, it is important to consider what happens in nature to affect the quality of water (contamination) and what man has superimposed on this (pollution).

New Words and Expressions

germinate ['dʒə:mineit]	v.	(使) 发芽，萌芽
alarming [ə'lɑ:miŋ]	a.	令人注目的
assume* [ə'sju:m]	vt.	呈现（某种形式）
chaos ['keiɔs]	n.	混乱，泛滥
Ethiopia [i:θi'əupiə]	n.	埃塞俄比亚
Bangladesh [ˌbɑ:ŋglə'deʃ]	n.	孟加拉国
urbanization [əbənai'zeiʃn]	n.	都市化
urban ['ə:bən]	a.	城市的
outstrip [aut'strip]	vt.	超越，胜过
effluent ['efluənt]	n.	污水，废水
epidemic [epi'demik]	n.	流行病，时疫
trace [treis]	n.	痕量，微量
trace metals		微量金属
monitor ['mɔnitə]	v.	检验（放射性污染物）
be exposed to		成为……受害者
bacteriology [bækˌtiəri'ɔlədʒi]	n.	细菌学
discharge [dis'tʃɑ:dʒ]	n.	排泄（水气），排泄物
annual ['ænjuəl]	a.	一年一度的，每年的
typhoid ['taifɔid]	n.	伤寒
cholera ['kɔlərə]	n.	霍乱
round [raund]	n.	循环，周期
eradicate [i'rædikeit]	vt.	根除，杜绝
assess [ə'ses]	vt.	估计，确定

lay down			制定，提出
recommendation	[rekəmen'deiʃən]	n.	建议，劝告
guideline *	['gaidlain]	n.	准则
reverse	[ri'və:s]	v.	扭转
superimpose	['sju:pərim'pəuz]	vt.	添加，附加

Notes

① …, from desert plants…to man himself…说明 all living things，其后分别跟了一个定语从句，修饰 desert plants 和 man himself.

② …the plants and animals…adequate water supply.
此句中的 the plants and animals 的谓语是 flourished; he required for food 是 the plants and animals 的定语从句。

③ This has resulted in …excessive amounts of trace metals, …
…resulted in 后有两个较长的介词宾语 many rivers and water courses… 和 and the population of towns and villages…。第二个宾语分为两部分，其中第二部分 to excessive amounts of trace metals 前省略了 becoming exposed.

Exercises

Reading Comprehension

Ⅰ. Say whether the following statements are True (T) or False (F) according to the text.

1. Desert plants always germinate and flower briefly because they get used to the climate of the desert. ( )
2. Without the presence of water, the environment in which modern man lives could not have developed as we now know it. ( )
3. Because technology developed faster than the science, pollution began. ( )
4. People do not know that excessive amounts of trace metals are harmful to human beings until recently. ( )
5. For thousands of years, man has been aware of his need of adequate quality of water. ( )
6. Typhoid and cholera regularly caused many people to die who were dependent on a polluted river for water. ( )
7. Before the mid-nineteenth century, people knew little about the causes of the epidemics of water-borne diseases. ( )
8. The recently available equipment makes it possible for man to concern over lead in the environment. ( )

9. Now human race is fully aware of the gravity of their mistakes in the misuse of water. (   )

10. All the water on the earth is generally available to man for purposes of health, food. (   )

II. Identify main ideas from each paragraph by matching the following ideas with their appropriate paragraph numbers.

    A. Realizing his mistakes in the misuse of water, man begins to take measures. (4)

    B. As urbanization and pollution commenced, man slowly realized the need for water of adequate quality. (3)

    C. The recent available equipment makes it possible to measure lead and to assess its effect. (7)

    D. The lack of knowledge in the third world leads to annual rounds of epidemics. (6)

    E. Man comes to know the importance of adequate water supply. (5)

Vocabulary

I. fill in the blanks with the verbs given below, change the forms if necessary.

| commence | outstrip | survive | assess | affect |
| germinate | assume | eradicate | measure | appreciate |

1. You can _____ these beans by soaking them in water and planting them.
2. We shall be able to _____ literary works better if we have some knowledge of stylistics.
3. Although the movement through some parts of the cycle may be relatively rapid, complete recycling of ground water must often _____ in geologic time.
4. The presence of water _____ the environment in which we live.
5. With the development of the science and bacteriology, people _____ to know the causes of many water-borne epidemics.
6. Yollow fever _____ in many countries.
7. The value of the property _____ at $30,000.
8. The developed countries _____ the developing countries in controlling water pollution.
9. Ancient farming methods still _____ in the Middle East.
10. He unconsciously _____ a look of surprise when he heard the news.

II. Complete each of the following statements with one of the four choices given below.

1. The reckless _____ of industry effluents into the river caused annual rounds of epidemics.

    A. disburden   B. discard   C. disarrange   D. discharge

2. I've _____ finished my book, only having a few changes to make in writing.
   A. virtually   B. perfectly   C. normally   D. accurately
3. We should see the _____ as well as the obverse of the urbanization.
   A. backward   B. disadvantage   C. shortcoming   D. reverse
4. All living things are _____ water to survive.
   A. independent of   B. dependent on   C. center on   D. revolved around
5. Very few plants will _____ without water.
   A. Flourish   B. flush   C. flash   D. flesh

Reading Material A

The Hydrologic Cycle

In nature, water is constantly changing from one state to another. The heat of the sun evaporates water from land and water surfaces. This water vapor (a gas), being lighter than air, rises until it reaches the cold upper air where it condenses into clouds. Clouds drift around according to the direction of the wind until they strike a colder atmosphere. At this point the water further condenses and falls to the earth as rain, sleet, or snow, thus completing the hydrologic cycle.

The complete hydrologic cycle, however, is much more complex. The atmosphere gains water vapor by evaporation not only from the oceans but also from lakes, rivers, and other water bodies, and from moist ground surfaces. Water vapor also is gained by sublimation from snowfields and by transpiration from vegetation and trees.

Water precipitation may follow various routes. Much of the precipitation from the atmosphere falls directly on the oceans. Of the water that does fall over land areas, some is caught by vegetation or evaporates before reaching the ground,① some is locked up in snowfields or icefields for periods ranging from a season to many thousands of years, and some is retarded by storage in reservoirs, in the ground, in chemical compounds, and in vegetation and animal life.

Because water is absolutely necessary for sustaining life and is of great importance in industry, men have tried in many ways to control the hydrologic cycle to their own advantage.② An obvious example is the storage of water behind dams in reservoirs, in climates where there are excesses and deficits of precipitation (with respect to water needs) at different times in the year. Another method is the attempt to increase or decrease natural precipitation by injecting particles of dry ice or silver iodide into clouds. This kind of weather modification has had limited success thus far. But many meteorologists believe that a significant control of precipitation can be achieved in the future.

Other attempts to influence the hydrologic cycle include the contour plowing of sloping farmlands to slow down runoff and permit more water to percolate into the ground, the construction of dikes to prevent floods and so on.③ The reuse of water before it returns to the sea is another common practice. Various water supply systems that obtain their water from rivers may recycle it several times (with purification) before it finally reaches the rivers mouth.

Men also attempt to predict the effects of events in the course of the hydrologic cycle. Thus, the meteorologist forecasts the amount and intensity of precipitation in a watershed, and the hydrologist forecasts the volume of runoff.

Notes

①Of the water that does fall…before reaching the ground, …
那些落向陆地的水,一部分被植物吸收或在落到地面之前就被蒸发,……
②因为维持生命必须有水,而且水在工业上也很重要,所以人们已试用许多方法控制水循环,使水为人类服务。
③其它影响水循环的努力包括：沿等高线耕作梯田,使水流减速,以便使更多的水渗入地下；以及修筑堤坝,防止水患等等。

Reading Material B

The Hydrologic Cycle and Water Quality

Water is one of the most abundant compounds found in nature, covering approximately three-fourths of the surface of the earth. In spite of this apparent abundance, several factors serve to limit the amount of water available for human use. It is well known that over 97 percent of the total water supply is contained in the oceans and other saline bodies of water and is not readily usable for most purposes. Of the remaining 3 percent, a little over 2 percent is tied up in ice caps and glaciers and along with atmospheric and soil moisture, is inaccessible. Thus, for their general livelihood and the support of their varied technical and agricultural activities, humans must depend upon the remaining 0.62 percent found in freshwater lakes, rivers, and groundwater supplies.

water is in a constant state of motion. Atmospheric water condenses and falls to the earth as rain, snow, or some other form of precipitation. Once on the earth's surface, water flows into streams, lakes, and eventually the oceans, or percolates through the soil and into aquifers that eventually discharge into surface waters. .① Through evaporation from surface waters or by evapotranspiration from plants, water molecules return to the atmosphere to repeat the cycle. Although the movement through some parts of the cycle may be relatively rapid, complete recycling of groundwater must often be measured in geologic time.

Water in nature is most nearly pure in its evaporation state. Because the very act of condensation usually requires a surface, or nuclei, water may acquire impurities at the very moment of condensation. Additional impurities are added as the liquid water travels through the remainder of the hydrologic cycle and comes into contact with materials in the air and on or beneath the surface of the earth. Human activities contribute further impurities in the form of industrial and domestic wastes, agricultural chemicals, and other, less obvious contaminants. Ultimately, these impure waters will complete the hydrologic cycle and return to the atmosphere as relatively pure water molecules. However, it is water quality in the intermediate stage which is of greatest concern because it is the quality at this stage that will affect human use of the water. ②

The impurities accumulated by water throughout the hydrologic cycle and as a result of human activities may be in both suspended and dissolved form③. Suspended material consists of particles larger than molecular size that are suspended by buoyant and viscous forces within the water. Dissolved material consists of molecules or ions that are held by the molecular structure of water. Colloids are very small particles that technically are suspended but often exhibit many of the characteristics of dissolved substances.

Water pollution may be defined as the presence in water of impurities in such quantity and of such nature as to impair the use of the water for a stated purpose. Thus the definition of water quality is predicted on the intended use of the water, and a gross determination of the quantity of and dissolved impurities, while useful in some cases, is not sufficient to completely define water quality. Many parameters have evolved that qualitatively reflect the impact that various impurities have on selected water uses④. Analytical procedures have been developed that quantitatively measure these parameters. Standard Methods for the Examination of Water and Wastewater has been the authoritative standard for test procedures for many years.

Notes

①一旦落到地面，水便流入河流、湖泊，最终汇入海洋；或者渗过土壤进入含水层，最终排入地面水中。
②然而，中间阶段的水质最为重要，因为这一阶段的水质将会影响人类对水的利用。
③整个水循环过程中所积累的杂质，以及人类各种活动所引入的污物，可在水中以悬浮和溶解形式出现。
④已有许多参数能定性地反映各种杂质对水的某些用途的影响。

UNIT FOUR

Text   The Purification of Water

[1]　　Sea water can be used for a supply of potable (or drinkable) water if it can be separated from the salt dissolved in it. The most direct way to do this is to distil it——turn it into steam, and then condense the steam. In the past, distillation has always been too expensive, but a great deal of success in cheapening the process has been achieved in the last few years. Some clever ideas have been thought out to do this.

[2]　　Another method of getting rid of salt is by electro-dialysis. This is an electrical method which is most promising when the water is brackish. Brackish water is salty, but does not have as much salt as the sea; for instance, it will be found some way up a river estuary① where sea and river water are mixed. A third method is to make the separation by freezing, the ice being almost pure; while a fourth method, which relies on high pressure, is called reverse osmosis.

[3]　　Returning to the rivers, a method of using their water which has been much discussed is the estuarine barrage. The mouth of the river is dammed and a freshwater lake created behind the dam. The Zuider Zee dam in Holland is an example.

[4]　　Now that the epidemics which water-borne diseases can cause are understood, water supplies are organized to prevent them. This means treating the water, and continually testing it to make sure that the treatment is effective and remains effective all the time. The first aim is to sterilize it (to kill any disease-carrying organisms it may contain). But the law demands more than that, and requires all water undertakings② to provide a supply of wholesome water. "Wholesome" means more than simply "not injurious": it means "promoting or conducive to health". So the chemical constituents of the water may be changed to improve its drinking quality.

[5]　　The first principle of all water treatment is to start with the best, purest water available. Then it must be brought up to standards which make it always fit to drink.

[6]　　For a normal public supply of water, there are several reasons for treating the water to purify it. First, there is turbidity. Turbid water has small particles of solids suspended in it, so it will be cloudy or muddy to look at. Then there is colour, and colour is not the same as turbidity. A clear water can still have colour if, for example, iron salts are dissolved in it; but wholesome water should be colourless. Purification should also remove taste and odour, and it may be necessary to remove the algae which grow in water-especially in a reservoir.

[7]　　Then, most important of all, the water must be made free from contamination from sewage,③ or free from pathogens-those organisms which carry disease. This is tested by measuring the water's freedom from certain bacteria.

[8]　　Treatment designed to change polluted water to a potable water supply usually involves

the following steps:

[9]　　Sedimentation, with or without the use of a chemical flocculating agent, results in a settling out of the coarse particles that tend to carry down bacteria and similar smaller particles.

[10]　　The water may then be passed through fairly deep sand filters. The floc is caught in the sand and forms a rather efficient filter removing most of the organic particles and bacteria.

[11]　　After filtration, water is greatly improved in quality, appearance, and sanitary properties, but it is generally not entirely free from bacteria. Therefore the water is generally chlorinated.

New Words and Expressions

distil [dis'til]	v.	蒸馏
distillation [disti'leiʃən]	n.	蒸馏法
electrodialysis [i'lektrəudai'ælisis]	n.	电渗析
brackish ['brækiʃ]	a.	稍咸的
estuary ['estjuəri]	n.	河口，海湾
osmosis [ɔz'məusis]	n.	渗透性
estuarine ['estjuərain]	a.	河口的，港湾的
barrage ['bɑːridʒ]	n.	拦河坝
the Zuider Zee dam		（荷兰）须德海堤坝
sterilize ['sterilaiz]	vt.	消毒，杀菌
wholesome ['həulsəm]	a.	卫生的，有益于健康的
injurious [in'dʒuəriəs]	a.	有害的
conducive [kəns'djuːsiv]	a.	有助于……的，促进的
be conducive to		对……有益的
be brought up to		被（使）……达到
constituent [kəns'titjuənt]	n.	组成物，构成物
turbid ['təːbid]	a.	混浊的，混乱的
pathogen ['pæθədʒiːn]	n.	病原体，病菌
sedimentation [sedimen'teiʃən]	n.	沉积法，沉积作用
flocculate ['flɔkjuleit]	v.	絮凝，绒聚
flocculating agent		絮凝剂
settling ['setliŋ]	n.	沉淀
settling out		沉淀出来
coarse [kɔːs]	a.	粗粒的，大的
filter ['filtə]	v.; n.	过滤，过滤器、池等
floc [flɔk]	n.	絮体，絮凝物体
filtration [fil'treiʃən]	n.	过滤，滤清

| chlorinate ['klɔːrineit] | vt. | 用氯消毒 |
| sanitary properties | | 卫生系数（性能，特点等） |

Notes

①…it will be found some way up a river estuary…
  up：顺或沿着…而上。这里指沿河口向上一段处。
②But the law demands…all water undertakings…
  water undertaking 意为：any company or public board that undertakes to supply water. 任何承担供水的部门或公司。
③Then, most important of all…free from contamination from sewage,…
  free from 免遭，免受。from sewage 作定语，修饰 contamination 意为污水的污染。

Exercises

Reading Comprehension

Ⅰ. Say whether the following statements are True (T) or False (F) according to the text.
  1. People still can't find ways to cheapen distillation. ( )
  2. There are four ways to get rid of salt from sea water, distillation being the most widely used one. ( )
  3. Brackish water is salty and has as much salt as the sea water. ( )
  4. The Zuider Zee dam in Holland is cited as one of the widely accepted methods of using water. ( )
  5. The law demands any company that undertakes to supply water should provide wholesome water. ( )
  6. Wholesome water is one kind of water which has only been sterilized. ( )
  7. Purified water should be no taste, no odour, no turbidity but sometimes colourful. ( )
  8. When water is greatly improved in quality, appearance, and sanitary properties, it is generally free from bacteria. ( )
  9. Treatment designed to change polluted water to a potable water supply usually involves three steps. ( )
  10. During sedimentation, the coarse particles can carry down some bacteria and similar smaller particles but not whole. ( )

Ⅱ. Identify main ideas from each paragraph by matching the following ideas with their appropriate paragraph numbers.
  A. According to the law, water undertakings should (1)

provide a supply of wholesome water.

B. Most important of all, water must be made (2)
free from pathogens.

C. Distillation is the most direct but rather expensive (4)
way to separate salt from sea water.

D. Several reasons for treating the water to (7)
purify it.

E. Some other ways to get rid of salt from sea (6)
water

Vocabulary

I. fill in the blanks with the words given below, change the form if necessary.

| promote | design | organize | remove | treat |
| sterilize | dissolve | create | suspend | mix |

1. The problem of providing a safe water supply has become more and more acute in recent years because of the vast amount of waste _____ by industrial processes.
2. People's concern over environment pollution has increased the demand that waste water should _____ to the fullest degree possible before it is returned to the environment.
3. Water may be filtered to remove _____ impurities, aerated to remove dissolved gases.
4. Fish and aquatic life depend on _____ oxygen.
5. More and more treatment plants _____ and built to purify water before it is released back into the environment.
6. Water is passed through a filter that consists of a bed of sand or gravel, which _____ a large proportion of the solids that might otherwise contaminate the supply.
7. You can't _____ oil with water.
8. The young army officer _____ to the rank of captain.
9. All workmen must _____ into a common union to abolish exploitation.
10. As all the bacteria may not yet have been removed from the water, it must still _____.

II. Complete each of the following statements with one of the four choices given below.
1. You'll a see a lot of _____ if you study some dirty water under the microscope.
   A. organs   B. organisms   C. organists   D. organizations
2. Certain amount of trace metals are _____ to a man's health.
   A. noxious   B. profitable   C. harmful   D. conducive
3. All water has the _____ of changing from one form to another.
   A. quality   B. essence   C. property   D. individuality
4. His clothes were made of _____ material.
   A. coarse   B. rough   C. crude   D. coach

5. An _____ is the tidal mouth of a great river.
   A. epigraph   B. episode   C. estuary   D. eternity

Reading Material A

Softening of Water

Certain materials in water react with soap, causing a precipitation which appears as a scum or curd on the water surface. Until enough soap has been dissolved to react with all these materials, no lather can be formed. A water which behaves like this is said to be "hard". When synthetic detergents are used instead of soap, the inconvenience of a hard water is not so strongly felt, because the detergents do not cause a precipitation of the hardness compounds. Nevertheless there are still many objections to a hard water,① the principal one being that when the water is heated in boilers and heating systems, the hardness compounds precipitate to form a hard scale on the surface of the boiler and the interior of pipes. The portion of the total hardness which is deposited when water is boiled is called "temporary hardness"; the remainder is called "permanent hardness". We see that calcium and magnesium are the cause of hardness, the bicarbonates producing temporary hardness, the sulphates and chlorides permanent hardness.

The hardness of a water creates no defect of palatability——on the contrary many people consider that the sparkling clear hard waters obtained from the chalk are second to none for drinking.

Hardness can be measured by the "soap destroying power" of a water, but more precisely by the total of the hardness producing constituents expressed in the chemically equivalent amount of calcium carbonate ($CaCO_3$).② Hardness has also been measured in the past as "degrees Clarke" which in fact are grains per gallon or parts per 70 000. Thus 100 ppm. hardness is equivalent to 7 degrees Clarke.③ Usual ranges of the natural hardness of raw waters are given in Table 1.

Table 1

Moorland catchments	10 to 50 ppm.
Shallow clays and gravels	Varying
Sandstones	100 to 300 ppm.
Chalk	200 to 300 ppm.
Oolitic and carboniferous limestones	200 to 300 ppm.
Magnesium limestones	400 to 500 ppm.

There are many individual cases, in all but the first category, giving extreme hardness figures of 800 to 1 000 ppm. The usual cause of a water being excessively hard is that a high percentage of the hardness is permanent. In the majority of waters the biggest portion of the hardness is temporary.

There are two different methods available for changing a hard water into a soft water. In the first method we add chemicals (lime and soda) to the water which change the hardness compounds so that they become insoluble and precipitate, and the water is then filtered through rapid gravity filters. In the second method we change the nature of the hardness compounds in a "base-exchange" softener so that they do not react with soap and the water therefore appears soft.

The difference between these two methods should be noticed. In the former process of chemical addition we remove the hardness compounds; in the latter process we change them. The result of this is that the total dissolved solids (i. e. the total impurities) are reduced with the lime and soda process, but they are not reduced when the base-exchange method of softening is used. This difference is of importance to many industrial users of water who wish to have as pure a water as possible whatever the constituents are. We shall later show how a double base-exchange process of softening can produce a water as pure as distilled water.

Notes

①many objections to a hard water 硬水的许多缺点。
②expressed in the chemically equivalent amount of calcium carbonate ($CaCO_3$)
   甲碳酸钙的化学当量表示
③硬度过去也被测定为'克拉克度',它实际上是用格令/加仑或七万分之几表示。这样,100 ppm. 硬度就等于7克拉克度。

Reading Material B

Softening of Water

Sky water becomes "hard" by addition of minerals which are dissolved as the water runs over the surface or percolates underground. Hardness can become a source of considerable expense to the consumer unless it is reduced by softening.

Water-softening processes for municipal plants are either the cold lime-soda process, the cation-exchange process (formerly called the zeolite process) or a combination of the two.① In the cold lime-soda process, the steps are usually: addition of chemicals (generally lime and soda ash), mixing, sedimentation in basins for the reaction to take place, rapid sand filtration, and recarbonation to prevent the formation of incrustants and scale.② If the water were not recarbonated (by diffusing carbon dioxide gas through it, to restore the carbon dioxide removed by the reaction with lime) the water would be unstable as to the solubility of carbonates and the corrosion of metals. The lime-soda process involves the handling of dusty lime, the deposal of great quantities of sludge, and expert supervision of recarbonation. If the recarbonation is not properly done, the sand, gravel, and equipment in the filters, and the pipes in the distribution system, will accumulate coatings of carbonates of calcium and magnesium.

The cation-exchange softener is the most widely used type in municipalities, industries, and homes. In industry and homes, a water of zero hardness is produced, while in municipalities, completely softened water is mixed with hard water, to produce a water of tolerable hardness. The softener occupies comparatively little space, and is simple to operate. A cation-exchange water softener consists essentially of a container (gravity or pressure type) for the bed of exchange material, and piping and appurtenances for passing water through that material in one direction for softening the water, and in the reverse direction for the regeneration of the bed. In the reverse flow, the water carries brine. There is also required a storage bin for the salt, and a tank for saturated salt brine. The principle of this proess lies in the ability of certain sodium compounds, which are insoluble, to exchange cations with other substances in the water.③ When a hard water is passed through a sodium cation exchanger, the calcium and magnesium in the hard water are replaced by sodium from the exchanger. Since the action is reversible, the "exhausted" cation exchanger can be "regenerated", with a solution of common salt, once all the readily replaceable sodium has been exchanged for calcium and magnesium from the hard water. In regeneration, The calcium and magnesium of the exhausted cation exchangers are replaced with a fresh supply of sodium from the regenerating brine unit. Then, after washing with water to free it of brine, the exchange material in the filter is in condition to soften a fresh supply of hard water.

Corrosion may be an incidental result of cation-exchange softening, unless provision is made to guard against it.④ Water softened by this process is not in itself corrosive, but the absence of magnesium and calcium compounds prevents the formation of a coating based on alkaline hard water which protects the metal from attack by oxygen, the real corrosive agent. To protect pipelines in distribution systems, it is therefore advisable to mix the softened water with the raw, or make such adjustments to the pH and alkalinity as will produce substantial saturation with calcium carbonate.

Notes

① 对于城市给水厂来说，水的软化有冷石灰—苏打法和阳离子交换法（旧称沸石软化法），或者两种方法合并使用。

② …addition of chemicals …to prevent the formation of incrustants and scale。
投加化学剂（一般为石灰和苏打粉）；混合；在池内产生反应沉淀；快砂池过滤，以及为防止结垢的再碳化过程。

③ 该工艺过程的原理是：某些不可溶钠化合物能与水中其它物质中的阳离子交换。

④ 如果不采取预防措施，那么用阳离子交换来软化水质可能产生的一个附带结果是腐蚀。

UNIT FIVE

Text   Basic Factors in Water Analysis

Colour

[1]   Colour is due to the presence of colloidal organic matter in solution or in suspension. There is no relation between the colour and the quantity of organic matter, as the latter may be coloured or not.

[2]   Water which is coloured is unpleasant when used for domestic purposes, and particularly for drinking, as it always gives rise to doubts regarding its portability.[①] Certain industries require water to be quite free from colour which might affect the products manufactured and detract from their quality; examples are the paper, rayon, cellulose, starch, and dyeing industries. Colour removal is effected by coagulation.

Odour and Taste

[3]   Odours and tastes are generally caused by the presence of secretions introduced into the water by organisms which live in the water, such as algae and fungi, etc.[②] Certain chemical products in small quantities also give of funpleasant odours. This is the case with phenols which, when combined with chlorine, form the very malodorous chlorophenols. Unpleasant tastes are not considered to be important from the health point of view, but they are extremely objectionable in drinking water.

[4]   Unpleasant tastes are combated by break-point chlorination, by activ ated carbon, by chlorine dioxide, and by ozone. All water samples, from whatever source, have their own particular taste due to the salts and gases dissolved in them.

Turbidity

[5]   Turbidity gives an idea of the content of matter in suspension. The turbidity may be expressed in terms of silica by comparing its transparency with an artificial suspension of silica. It expresses the concentration of finely divided suspended matter which may eventually settleafter variable periods of time, such substances being clay, fine sand, limestone particles, etc.[③] The measurement of turbidity by drops of mastic is particularly useful in ascertaining the content of the colloidal particleswhich will not settle and which cannot be filtered. That is why it is essential to carry out this test after filtering the liquid through paper in order to eliminate the influence of large particles, and thus to know exactly the extent of the turbidity due to the colloidal substances which are the most frequent causes of colour.[④]

[6]　　Turbidity is always unpleasant in drinking water.

Waters containing suspended matter which may eventually settle always cause difficulty due to the formation of deposits in pipes and tanks.

[7]　　Lastly, industries in which the water comes into contact with the manufactured products always demand clear water while often permitting a certain colloidal turbidity.

[8]　　Turbidity is related to transparency.

A turbidity value of less than 10 drops of mastic gives good transparency through a depth of 4 metres but drinking waters generally require a turbidity value of less than 4 drops.

[9]　　Colloidal turbidity can be eliminated only by coagulation.

As a general rule the water is clarified in a settling tank with or with out coagulation, and this process is followed by filtration.

[10]　　Waters containing less than 20 p.p.m. of suspended matter which can be coalesced and decolorized by the use of not more than 20 p.p.m. of coagulant can be treated by direct filtration.

[11]　　Knowledge of turbidity is an indispensable factor in water treatment.

Conductivity or Resistivity

[12]　　Conductivity depends on the concentration of dissolved solid. Its measurement, which is quite an easy matter, gives some idea as to the salt concentration in the water. Knowledge of this factor is particularly useful for the periodic checking of a given water, as immediate indication of variations in composition is obtained.

Temperature

[13]　　The test for temperature of water has no practical meaning in the sense that it is not possible to give any treatment to control the temperature in any water supply project.[5] The temperature of water to be supplied from storage reservoir depends on the depth from which it is drawn. The desirable temperature of potable water is 10°C which temperature of 25°C is considered to be objectionable.

[14]　　It should however be noted that changes in temperature of water from its source to the mains may be helpful in detecting the unsuspected source of pollution.[6] Also, the multiplication of bacteria in the waters is more rapid at higher temperature than in the waters at lower temperature. Hence when waters with a temperature of about 15°C are collected for bacteriological analysis, they should be cooled down as quickly as possible. It should further be remembered that the air temperature at the time of taking the water sample should always be recorded.

pH Value

[15]   pH values indicate whether the water is acid or alkaline. pH values less than 7 show a tendency towards acidity. Values above 7 indicate a tendency towards alkalinity.

[16]   They have no health significance, but represent a very important factor in determining the corrosive action of a water.

[17]   The regular measurement of the pH value is an essential factor in water treatment practice. In particular it plays an important part in the efficiency of the coagulation process.

New Words and Expressions

colloidal [kə'lɔidl]	a.	胶体（状，质）的
suspension * [səs'penʃən]	n.	悬浮（液），悬胶（体）
portability [pəutə'biliti]	n.	可饮用
detract * [di'trækt]	v.	降低，减损
rayon ['reiɔn]	n.	人造丝
cellulose ['seljuləuz]	n.	纤维素
starch [stɑ:tʃ]	n.	淀粉
odour ['əudə]	n.	气味，臭气
secretion [si'kri:ʃən]	n.	分泌液
fungi [fʌŋgai]	n.	真菌
phenol ['fi:nɔl]	n.	（苯）酚
chlorine * ['klɔ:ri:n]	n.	氯（气）
malodorous [mæ'ləudərəs]	a.	恶臭的
chlorophenols ['klɔ:rə'fi:nəlz]	n.	氯酚
objectionable * [əb'dʒekʃənəbl]	a.	讨厌的，有异议的
combat * ['kɔmbət]	v.	和……作斗争，反对
break-point chlorination		折点加氯
activated carbon		活性炭
chlorine dioxide		二氧化氯
ozone ['əuzəun]	n.	臭氧
silica * ['silikə]	n.	二氧化硅
transparency [træns'pɛərənsi]	n.	透明（性，度）
mastic ['mæstik]	n.	胶粘剂
ascertain * [æsə'tein]	vt.	确定，查明
p.p.m. = parts per million		百万分之（几）
coalesce [kəu'les]	vi.	凝聚

decolorize [diːˈkʌləraiz]		vt.	漂白
conductivity * [kɔndʌkˈtiviti]		n.	传导性
resistivity * [rizisˈtiviti]		n.	电阻性
periodic * [piəriˈɔdik]		a.	定期的
unsuspected [ˈʌnsəsˈpektid]		a.	未知的
multiplication * [ˌmʌltipliˈkeiʃən]		n.	增加，乘
bacteriological [bækˌtiəriəˈlɔdʒikəl]		a.	细菌学的
alkaline [ˈælkəlain]		n.; a.	碱性；碱性的
acidity [əˈsiditi]		n.	酸性（度）
alkalinity [ælkəˈliniti]		n.	（强）碱性
corrosive * [kəˈrəusiv]		a.	腐蚀的

Notes

①Water which is coloured is … doubts regarding its portability.

which is coloured 是定语从句，修饰名词 water。

when used … for drinking 是过去分词短语，在句中作时间状语。

as 引导的从句是原因状语从句，句中"give rise to"意为"引起，造成"。

②Odours and tastes are generally … algae and fungi, etc.

introduced into the water by organisms 是过去分词短语，作定语，修饰 secretions.

which live in the water, such as algae and fungi, etc. 是定语从句，修饰 organisms. 句中 such as 引导插入语，意为"诸如藻类和真菌等"。

③It expresses the concentration … limestone particles, etc.

It 指 the turbidity。finely divided suspended matter 意为"细微的悬浮物质"。which may eventually settle after variable periods of time 是定语从句，修饰 matter。

such substances being clay, fine… 是独立主格，插入语，补充说明 finely divided suspended matter.

④This is why … causes of colour.

why 引导的从句是表语从句。

in order to elimination … and thus to know 两个均为不定式，作目的状语。which are the most frequent causes of colour 是定语从句，修饰 colloidal substances.

⑤The test for temperature of water … in any water supply project in the sense that 意为"从某种意义上说"。

in the sense that … project 是插入语，对全句作补充说明。

⑥It should however be noted that changes in … source of pollution that 引导出宾语从句，在该从句中 changes 为主语，may be helpful 为谓语。

Exercises

Reading Comprehension

I. Say whether the following statements are True (T) or False (F) according to the text.
  1. There is colour in the water because of the presence of colloidal organic matter in solution or in suspension. ( )
  2. The colour has relation to the quantity of organic matter, as the organic matter may be coloured or not. ( )
  3. Although tastes are not considered to be important from the health point of view, they are unpleasant for drinking water. ( )
  4. Turbidity refers to the content of the colloidal matter in suspension. ( )
  5. Turbidity is related to transparency, so colloidal turbidity can be eliminated only by ordinary filtration. ( )
  6. Knowing the knowledge of turbidity is of great importance in water treatment. ( )
  7. As conductivity depends on the concentration of dissolved solids, the salt concentration in the water can be obtained by measuring conductivity. ( )
  8. The temperature of water to be supplied from storage reservoir depends on the quantity which it is drawn. ( )
  9. The desirable temperature of potable water is 25 ℃ while temperature of 10 ℃ is considered to be objectionable. ( )
  10. pH values are no matter to health, so the regular measurement of the pH value is unnecessary in water treatment practice. ( )

II. Choose the best answer according to the text.
  1. The water which is quite free from colour is required by certain industries, such as _____.
     A. the paper industry   B. the starch industry
     C. the dyeing industry   D. All of the above
  2. _____ are generally due to the secretions which algae and fungi introduce into the water.
     A. colour   B. odours and tastes   C. turbidity   D. temperature
  3. Drinking waters generally require a turbidity value of _____.
     A. four drops   B. ten drops
     C. less than four drops   D. less than ten drops
  4. The multiplication of bacteria in the waters is more rapid _____.
     A. at higher temperature than at lower temperature
     B. at lower temperature than at higher temperature
     C. at low temperature than at high temperature

D. at high temperature than at low temperature
5. pH values indicate whether the water is acid or alkaline. pH values _____ show a tendency towards alkaline.
   A. less than 7   B. equal 7
   C. more than 7   D. none of the above

Vocabulary

I. Complete the following sentences with some of the words or expressions listed below, changing the form where necessary.

| clarify | secretion | deposit | ascertain | suspend |
| detract | eliminate | coalesce | corrosive | acidity |

1. The water which is coloured might affect the products manufactured and _____ from their quality.
2. It is well known that rust (锈) and acid (酸) are _____.
3. Suspended matter in the water may often be seen to settle and form _____ in pipes and tanks.
4. The measurement of turbidity by drops of mastic is particularly useful in _____ the content of the colloidal particles.
5. The water containing suspended matter is generally _____ in a settle tank with or without coagulation and then is filtered.

II. Complete each of the following statements with one of the four choices given below.
1. Coloured water is unpleasant when it is used for domestic purposes or certain industries. And colour removal is effected by _____.
   A. coagulation   B. decolorizing   C. filtration   D. clarifying
2. It is well known that hydrogen and oxygen _____ to form water.
   A. dissolve   B. coalesce   C. combine   D. clarify
3. The standard method of measuring _____ is with the Jackson Candle Turbidimeter (杰克逊烛光浊度计) first developed in 1900.
   A. temperature   B. turbidity   C. concentration D. pH value
4. Please carry out the test after _____ the liquid through paper in order to eliminate large particles.
   A. decolorizing   B. suspending   C. clarifying   D. filtering
5. Quantitative measurements of pollutants are obviously necessary before water pollution can be _____. Measurement of these pollutants is, however, fraught with difficulties.
   A. controlled   B. corrosive   C. settled   D. eliminated

Reading Material A

Water Testing

It is necessary to measure pollutants in water before water pollution can be controlled. However, measuring pollutants in water is fraught with many difficulties. ①

The first problem is that the specific materials responsible for the pollution are sometimes not know. The second difficulty is that these pollutants are generally at low concentrations, and very accurate methods of detection are therefore required.

Many of the pollutants are measured in terms of milligrams of the substance per liter of water (mg/l). This is a weight/volume measurement. In many older publications pollutants are measured as parts per million (ppm), a weight/weight parameter. If the liquid involved is water these two units are identical, since 1 millilitre of water weights 1 gram. Because of the possibility of some wastes not weighing the same as water, the ppm measure has been scrapped in favor of mg/l.

A third commonly used parameter is percent , a weigh / weight relationship . Obviously 10 000 ppm= 1 percent and this is equal to 10 000 mg/l only if 1ml = 1g.

The measure of water quality is generally in the follow aspect color and odor, solid, pH, dissolved oxygen, biochemical oxygen demand, chemical oxygen demand, total organic carbon, turbidity, nitrogen, phosphates etc.

Turbidity

Water which is not clear but is "dirty", in the sense that light transmission is inhibited, is known as turbid water. ② Turbidity can be caused by many materials. In the treatment of water for drinking purposes, turbidity is of great important factor because pathogenic organisms can hide on (or in) the tiny colloidal particles.

The standard method of measuring turbidity is with the Jackson Candle Turbidimeter first developed in 1900. It consists of a long flat-bottomed glass tube under which a candle is placed. The turbid water is poured into the glass tube until the outline of the flame is no longer visible. The centimeters of water in the tube are then measured and compared to the standard turbidity unit, which is:

1mg/l SiO_2 =1 unit of turbidity

Recent years have seen the development of electronic devices which measurelight scatter or transmittance. ③ These have completely replaced theantiquated Jackson Candle in the laboratory.

Color and odor

Color and odor are both important measurements in water treatment. Along with turbidity they are called the physical parameters of drinking water quality.

Color is measured by comparison with standards. Colored water made with potassium chloroplatinate when tinted with cobalt chloride closely resembles the color of many natural waters.[④] Where multicolored industrial wastes are involved, such color measurement is meaningless.

Odor is measured by successive dilution of sample with odor-free water until the odor is no longer detectable. This test is obviously subjective and depends entirely on the olfactory senses of the tester.

Solids

One of the main problems with wastewater treatment is that so much of wastewater is actually solid. The separation of these solids from the water is in fact one of the primary objectives of treatment.

Solids can be divided into two fractions: the dissolved solids and the suspended solids. The table salt is an example of dissolved solids while the sand would be measured as a suspended solid. The separation of suspended solids is by means of a special crucible. It has holes on the bottom on which a glass fiber filter is place. The sample is then drawn through the crucible with the aid of a vacuum. The suspended material is retained on the filter while the dissolved fraction passes through. If the initial dry weight of the crucible and filter are known, the subtraction of this from the total weight of crucible filter and the dried solids caught on the filter yields the weight of suspended solids, expressed as mg/L.

Total organic carbon

Since the ultimate oxidation of organic carbon is to CO_2, the total combustion of a sample will yield some significant information on the amount of organic carbon present in a wastewater sample. Without elaboration, this is done by allowing a little bit of the sample to be burned in a combustion tube and measuring the amount of CO_2 emitted[⑤]. This test is not widely used at present, mainly because of the expensive instrumentation required.

Notes

①be fraught with 意为"充满"。
　　全句意为"然而，这些污染物的测量都充满了困难。"
②in the sense that 意为"从某种意义上说。"

全句意为"不清结的有污染的水,从某种意义上说光传播受阻的水,被称作浑浊水。"

③本句中的主语省略,have seen 为谓语。

全句意为"近年来,又发明了用以测量光的散射和传播的电子装置。"

④when 在句中为 conj. 连接两个过去分词短语,意为"然后"。

全句意为"用氯铂酸钾制成,然后用氯化钴着色的有色的水,其颜色很接近天然水的颜色。"

⑤意为"可将少量样品放在燃烧管里燃烧,然后测定释放出来的二氧化碳,但这样做不够精确。"

Reading Material B

The General Physical-chemical Principle of Water

Prior to discussing natural, aquatic, and marine systems, it is necessary to discuss the chemical and physical properties of the constituents that comprise these systems. Although the waters of the world contain many, if not all, of the chemical elements known to man, these elements have many commonly shared characteristics.① Thus a consideration of the chemical and physical characteristics of these elements provides a convenient starting point for the study of water resources.

All matter in the world is composed of electrically neutral atoms, and all atoms are composed of smaller components termed subatomic particles. Although physicists have discovered over 30 subatomic particles, only 3 need be considered here: the proton, the neutron, and the electron.

The proton is a positively charged particle located in the center of the atom in a region termed the nucleus. The proton is a relatively stable particle and has an assigned relative weight of l. The neutron is also located in the nucleus, is neutral charged but unstable, and also has an assigned relative weight of l. Electrons are negatively charged, orbit the nucleus in a series of electron clouds, are relatively stable, and have an assigned relative weight of 1/1840th the weight of a proton or neutron. Since all atoms are electrically neutral, they must have the same number of electrons as protons in order to maintain electrical neutrality.② The sum of the weights of these subatomic particles gives each atom its characteristic weight, which is termed the gram atomic weight of that atom. Since it is impossible to weigh and/or work with individual atoms, chemists generally work with larger quantities, such as grams. To maintain a consistent relationship between atoms they use quantities termed moles. A mole of any substance is merely the gram atomic weight of that substance expressed in grams.

The number of protons contained in the nucleus of a particular atom, as well as the gram atomic weight of the atom, is conveniently determined from the Periodic Chart. Note that each atom on the chart is represented by a symbol and that numbers appear both above and below the symbol for each atom.③ The number directly below the symbol represents the atomic weight of that element, while the number above the symbol gives the total number of protons contained within the nucleus. Since all atoms are electrically neutral, there must be an identical number of electrons circling about the nucleus in one or more electron clouds. For example, hydrogen is listed on the periodic chart as H. The number 1 indicated that the hydrogen atom has one proton in the nucleus and, hence, must have an electron cloud consisting of one electron. The lower number (1 008) is the gram atomic weight of the hydrogen atom. Thus if a chemist weighed out 1 008 grams (g) of hydrogen, I mole of hydrogen would be obtained.

Table 5-1 summarizes the characteristics of the subatomic particles. It is to be noted that the only basic difference among the various atoms is their size and weight, which is governed by the number of protons, electrons, and neutrons that comprise any given atom.④

Table 5-1

characteristics of subatomic particles				
Particle	Symbol	Charge	Relative Weight	Stability
Proton	+	Positive	1	Stable
Neutron	o	Neutral	1	Unstable
Electron	e-	Negative	1/1 840	Stable

Notes

①句中 if not all 为条件状语从句,省略了主句中相同的句子成分。
全句意为"尽管世界上各类水都含有许多(即使不是全部)为人们所知道的化学元素,但这些元素具有许多共同的特性。"
②句中 as 引出的定语从句(省略句),与主句中 the same 相呼应。as 在句中作宾语。
全句意为"因为所有的原子都是电中性的,所以原子一定具有与质子数目相同的电子数以保持电中性。"
③本句为祈使句。that 引出的两个从句都是谓语动词 note 的宾语从句。
全句意为"注意在周期表中,每一个原子符号的上下方都有数字。"
④句中 it 是形式主语,that 引出的句子是真实主语从句。
全句意为"值得注意的是,各种原子之间唯一的基本差别是它们的大小和重量,这取决于构成某给定原子的质子,电子和中子数目的多少。"

UNIT SIX

Text Water-supply Engineering

[1]   A water supply for a town usually includes a storage reservoir at the source of the supply, a pipeline from the storage reservoir to the distribution reservoir near the town, and finally the distribution pipes buried in the streets, taking the water to the houses, shops, factories and offices.① The main equipment is thus the two reservoirs and the pipeline between them. The function of the storage reservoir is keep enough water over one or several years to provide for all high demands in dry periods, and the distribution reservoir has the same function for the day or the week. The storage reservoir by its existence allows the supply sources to be smaller and less expensive. And the distribution reservoir similarly allows the pipeline and pumps to be smaller and cheaper than they would be if it did not exist.②

[2]   In the United States, some of whose cities have the largest water use in the world per person, the average use per person varies from 200 to 5 000 litres per day, averaging some 500 litres/day/person. But it must not be assumed that colder countries will eventually reach the same level of use, because much of the highest US demand comes from the water spent in summer on air conditioning equipment and the watering of gardens.

[3]   Water engineers must therefore study the water use per person (consumption per head) in their own country and choose a figure based on the most advanced community there.③ The chosen consumption per head must be multiplied by the estimated population at the date for which the supply is being planned, some thirty years ahead or more.④ The supply and storage equipment must be designed to be large enough for this period since neither of them is so easily extended as the distribution system. This can be extended as the need arises and as the houses are built.

[4]   Once the volume of the required yearly supply has been calculated and agreed with all concerned, including the fire department, it is important to make sure that it really is permanently obtainable from the catchment area proposed. The catchment area is the area which drains towards the supply, and the yearly amount of water drawn off to the storage reservoir cannot be more than the rainfall on the catchment area and should usually be very much smaller.

[5]   A water supply may be obtained from surface water (rain) or from underground water or both. Both are refilled by the rainfall, the surface water by the runoff, and the springs or wells by the water which enters the ground, the infiltration water. These two quantities, plus the evaporation water and the water used by the trees and plants, make up the total rainfall. Even if the community water supply includes all the springs as well as the surface water in the area, it still does not obtain all the rainfall because of evaporation and the needs of plant life.

[6]   It is therefore important to check the rainfall records and the runoff and infiltration val-

ues with the records of the stream flows and other local water information.⑤ Infiltration water, the rainfall which enters the ground and becomes ground water, can travel for long horizontal distances, and it may pass into or out of the catchment area. If the yearly water supply exceeds the yearly rainfall, the ground water level will generally fall and eventually it will become impossible to obtain the required supply. Another source will have to be found.

[7]   It is not essential to build a storage or impounding reservoir if the water can be stored in the ground, and this may often be possible. In face in the London area, where the water level in the chalk has been steadily falling for more than a century because of pumping, it has been suggested that further storage shall be not by the surface reservoirs which have been used until now,⑥ but by recharging the chalk with purified water through wells changed for the purpose.⑦

[8]   This practice of underground storage is being widely used by the gas industry in many countries. Gas is sent underground by compressors through wells into a sealed underground sand, limestone, or other porous formation at a time when the gas supply is large, to be stored until the demand is larger than the supply. These underground containers for gas are often hundreds of times as large as the largest gas tank in existence and have been found to be a cheap, practical, and safe way of storing gas.

New Words and Expressions

water-supply	a.	给水的
storage reservoir		蓄水库（池）
pipeline ['paiplain]	n.	管道（线）
distribution reservoir		配水库（池）
distribution system		配水系统（网）
distribution pipe		配水管道
to provide for		提供，作准备
high demands		高峰用水量
supply source		水源
come from		由于
air conditioning equipment		空调设备
water (supply) engineer		给水工程师
to be multiplied by		乘以
neither…is so easily…as…		都不能象……那样易于
concerned [kən'sə:nd]	a.	有关的
the fire department		消防部门
to make sure that		确保
obtainable * [əb'teinəbl]	a.	能得到的，能达到的

catchment ['kætʃmənt]		n.	集水（量），汇水
catchment area			集水区
rainfall ['reinfɔːl]		n.	降雨量
refill [riː'fil]		v.	再装（灌）满
runoff ['rʌn'ɔf]		n.	径流（量）
infiltration [infil'treiʃən]		n.	渗透（入）
infiltration water			渗透水
evaporation [iˌvæpə'reiʃən]		n.	蒸发
evaporation water			蒸发水
impounding [im'paundiŋ]		v.	贮（水）备灌溉用
impounding reservoir			蓄水池
recharge ['riː'tʃɑːdʒ]		v.	再装，再补充
purify ['pjuərifai]		v.	使纯净，使结净
compressor * [kəm'presə]		n.	压缩机
limestone ['laimstɔn]		n.	石灰石
porous * ['pɔːrəs]		a.	多孔的
formation [fɔː'meiʃən]		n.	地（岩）层
limestone formation			石灰岩层
porous formation			多孔岩层
hundreds of times as large as…			比……大几百倍

Notes

①taking the water … offices 是分词短语作定语用，说明 distribution pipes。

②The storage reservoir by its existence … it did not exist. by its existence 意为"由于蓄水库的存在"。

to be smaller and less expensive 为宾语 the supply source 的宾语补足语。than they would be if it did not exist 是比较状语从句，从句本身又是主从复合句。主句和从句的主语 they 和 it 分别代表 the pipeline and pumps 和 the distribution reservoir。谓语动词 would be 和 did not exist 均为虚拟语气，表示与事实不符。

③句中"country"作"地区"、"区域"解。

the most advanced community "最先进的地区"。

④The chosen consumption per head … some thirty years ahead or more. for which the supply is being planned 是限定性定语从句，修饰 the date. some thirty years ahead or more 为 the date 的同位语。some 在数词前作状语，意义相当于 about "约"、"大约"。

⑤It is therefore important to check … 句中 it 为形式主语。不定式短语 to check the rain fall … 为真正主语。

⑥it has been suggested that … 句中 it 为形式主语，that 引导主语从句。it has been suggested 译为主动语态"有人建议"。

⑦through wells changed for the purpose 直译:"通过为此而改变用途的井(指井不是为了取水,而是为了灌水)",今转译为:"而改为再向井内……而达到蓄水的目的"。

Exercises

Reading Comprehension

Ⅰ. Say whether the following statements are True (T) or False (F) according to the text.
1. A water supply for a city usually includes a storage reservoir and the distribution pipes carrying the water to the users. (   )
2. The function of the storage reservoir is different from that of the distribution reservoir. (   )
3. As the supply and storage equipment are difficult to be extended, they must be designed to be large enough. (   )
4. Before designing a water supply system, water engineers must study the consumption per head per day in the area. (   )
5. In some cities of the United States, the average water use per head per day is 5000 liters. (   )
6. If the yearly water supply can't exceed the yearly rainfall, the ground water level will generally fall. (   )
7. It is of great importance to check the rainfall records, the runoff and infiltration values with the records of stream flows and other local water information. (   )
8. The total rainfall consists of surface water and underground water. (   )
9. If the storage reservoir and the distribution reservoir exist, the supply sources and the pipeline will be smaller and cheaper. (   )
10. So far the practice of underground storage is impossible. (   )

Ⅱ. Choose the best answer according to the text.
1. The main equipment of a water supply is _____.
    A. a storage reservoir and a distribution reservoir
    B. two storage reservoirs and the pipeline between them
    C. two distribution reservoirs and the pipeline between them
    D. a storage reservoir, a distribution reservoir and the pipeline between them
2. The function of the storage reservoir is _____ to provide for all high demands in dry periods.
    A. to keep enough water over one or several days
    B. to keep enough water over one or several years
    C. to supply enough water over one or several weeks
    D. to supply enough water over one or several months
3. All the rainfall can't be obtained, because _____.

A. there will always be some loss due to evaporation and the needs of plant life

B. the rainfall enters the ground

C. it becomes the springs and wells

D. all the rainfall is evaporated and absorbed by the plants

4. If the yearly water supply exceeds the yearly rainfall, we will have to _____.

A. build another storage reservoir

B. bury more pipes in the streets

C. find another source of water supply

D. both A and B

5. It is not necessary to build a storage reservoir if _____.

A. the water can be taken to the users directly

B. the water can be stored in the ground

C. the water can be stored in the water tower

D. we build a high water tower

Vocabulary

I. Complete the following sentences with some of the words or expressions listed below, changing the form where necessary.

| supply | storage | travel | check | extend |
| obtain | provide | make up | make sure | base on |

1. Underground water may pass into or out of the catchment area and can _____ for long horizontal distance.

2. A water supply may be _____ from underground water as well as from surface water.

3. Water engineers must study the local information and choose a figure _____ the most advanced community there.

4. We consider it very important _____ the computing data with the result obtained in the experiment.

5. The surface water and underground water, plus the evaporation water and the water used by plants _____ the total rainfall.

II. Complete each of the following statements with one of the four choices given below.

1. A _____ reservoir is a reservoir near the source of water supply and used for keeping water in it.

A. pumped   B. storage   C. distribution   D. detention

2. The _____ pipes buried under the ground take the water to the houses, shops, factories, offices and all the users.

A. sewer （污水）   B. waste   C. distribution   D. spray （喷水）

3. The rainfall which enters the ground and becomes the ground water is called _____

water.

    A. infiltration   B. evaporation   C. surface   D. spring

4. Water engineers must multiply the chosen _____ per head by the estimated population.

    A. information   B. number   C. figure   D. consumption

5. The state _____ large sums of money for water conservancy projects （水利工程）.

    A. checks   B. calculates   C. provides   D. chooses

Reading Material A

Drainage, Sewerage and Sewage

Drainage is a general term applied to fluid flow along all pipes or open channels which take liquid wastes or rain water.① A land drain is usually a pipe buried in farm land but it may also be an open channel. In a dry, hot climate, drains are rarely needed, and irrigation channels or pipes bring water to the fields instead of taking it away.

Sewage, however, is rather different. It is the liquid, usually domestic waste, from a community, and must be carefully distinguished from sewerage.② Sewerage means mainly the pipes or drains which carry sewage but can include all sewage collection, treatment and removal.

In dry weather the sewage flow of any community is generally equal to the water quantity it uses (dry-weather flow) plus any water that leaks into the sewers from the ground and minus any sewage that leaks out from the sewers. The amount of water used by the community is therefore the figure used by the civil engineer when he is designing the sewage system for its minimum rate of flow.

Sewerage systems are either 'separate' or 'combined'.③ In separate systems the rainwater is passed through a different drain from the 'sanitary' sewer containing the sewage, and they are therefore more expensive in drains but the sewage treatment is easier. In a separate system, of course, the sewage flow is the dry-weather flow, though the hourly rate varies through the twenty-four hours from 50 per cent to 150 per cent of the average through the day.

Several house drains, usually of 10cm internal diameter and made of fired clay, flow into the street sewer which is of 15—23cm diameter. Several of these flow into a branch sewer, which joins first a sub-main and then a main sewer taking it to the treatment plant. From the plant the treated water flows out as effluent, which may be pure water, in a large pipe called the outfall to a river or the sea or to farms. A shaft called a manhole is provided at all sharp bends or junctions of sewers to give access in case of blockage.④ Storm sewers are those that carry any heavy rainfall.

A sewage system is designed for its flow in cubic metres / second and this can be obtained in part from the city water department as the amount of water used, and in part (for the future) from the following information: rainfall, population growth, city plans and zoning, and the probable future building. Great differences would be found between the quantities and types of flow from highly populated areas, wealthy housing areas, and commercial or industrial areas.

In a country district, particularly one with sandy soil, the sewage can be treated merely by spreading it over farm land, a method that is simple, and cheap in a district with a small population. Although the amount of solid matter in sewage is less than 0.1 per cent, the first task in the sewage treatment itself is to separate the solids from the liquid. Coarse solids are removed by racks, coarse filters or detritus tanks; floating solids are removed by skimming tanks, and fine solids by finer filters, sedimentation tanks, or contact aerators, or other treatments.⑤ The solids are then treated by digestion in Imhoff tanks or by de-watering, and removed by pumping or burning or dumped as fill on low-lying ground. Fluid sludge can be sold to farmers for spreading on their fields.

The water after further purification, which may include chlorination or oxidation by various means, flows off to river or the sea or (preferably) to the land, or for re-use as industrial water. Advanced purification of the effluent from a sewage plant can noticeably reduce the community's water demand and the costs of its water department.

An important measure of the strength of a sewage is its biochemical oxygen demand, expressed in milligrammes of oxygen taken in at a stated temperature in so many days.⑥ The chemical analysis of a sewage states this figure as well as the contents of solids, nitrogen, chlorides, and fats, etc. The total solids will include suspended, dissolved, and settleable, and may be volatile or fixed. The volatile solids content is another important measure of the sewage strength and shows how fast it is likely to rot.

Notes

①general term：通用明词 open channel：明渠 to take：容纳。
全句意为"排水是一个通用名词，凡沿着容纳废水或雨水的一切管道或明渠流动的液体均可用这一名词。"
②It 指 sewage. liquid 可不译出，以避免重复。
全句意为"它（指污水）通常是指来自居民区的生活污水，必须细心地将污水一词（sewage）与污水工程（sewerage）区分开来。"
③排水系统有'分流制'和'合流制'两种。
④shaft：竖井；manhole：检查井；sharp bends：急剧转弯。
give access：可供人进入；in case of：在发生……的情况下
全句意为"在污水管所有急剧转弯和联接点处，都设有一个竖井，称为检查井。在发生堵塞的情况下，可供人进出。"

⑤粗大的固体物质用格栅、粗滤池或沉渣池清除，漂浮的固体由撇渣池除去，细小的固体则用细滤池、沉淀池、接触式曝气池或其它处理方法除去。

⑥measure：指标（度量标准）；taken in = received 被消耗的，被吸收的。

全句意为"污水浓度的一项重要指标是生化耗氧量。它用在规定天数内，规定温度下所消耗的氧的毫克值来表示。"

Reading Material B

Water Supply

Water supply is a process by which water is provided for some use, e. g. , to home, factory or business. The term may also refer to the supply of water provided in this way. The stringency of the requirements that a supply of water must meet depends on the use to be made of it.① For example, water used to wash semiconductor material from which transistors are made must be extraordinarily pure. The more usual requirement, however, is that water be free enough of harmful bacteria, chemicals, and other contamination to be drinkable.② It is also desirable that water be free of substances that make its taste or appearance unpleasant.③ Water that is to be used for washing must be fairly free of salts of calcium and magnesium. Water containing much of these, also called hard water, interferes with the action of soap.

The basic source of water is rainfall, which collects in rivers and lakes, under the ground, and in artificial reservoirs. Water from under the ground is called groundwater and is tapped by means of wells. Most often water must be raised from a well by pumping. In some cases a well will draw water from a permeable rock layer called an aquifer in which the water is under pressure; such a well needs little or no pumping. Water that collects in rivers, lakes, or reservoirs is called surface water. Most large water supply systems draw surface water through special intake pipes or tunnels and transport it to the area of use through canals, tunnels, or pipelines, which are known as mains or aqueducts. These feed a system of smaller conduits or pipes that take the water to its place of use.

A complete water supply system is often known as a water-works. Sometimes the term is specifically applied to pumping stations, treatment stations, or storage facilities. Storage facilities are provided to reserve extra water for use when demand is high and, when necessary, to help maintain water pressure. Treatment stations are places in which water may be filtered to remove suspended impurities, aerated to remove dissolved gases, or disinfected with chlorine, ozone, ultraviolet light, or some other agent that kills harmful bacteria and microorganisms. Sometimes hard water is softened by a process that exchanges dissolved calcium and magnesium salts for sodium salts, which do not interfere with soap.④ Salts of iodine and fluorine, which are considered helpful in preventing goiter and tooth decay, are some times added to water in which they are lacking. Not all water supply systems are used to deliver drinking water.

Systems used for purposes such as irrigation and fire fighting operate in much the same way as systems for drinking water, but the water need not meet such high standards of purity.⑤ In most municipal systems hydrants are connected to the drinking water system except during period of extreme water shortage. Because many cities draw water from the same body into which they discharge sewage, proper sewage treatment has become increasingly essential to the preservation of supplies of useful water.

Notes

①句中 that 引出的定语从句，修饰 requirements；to be made of it 修饰 the use；it 代替 the supply of water。

全句意为"供水所必须满足的水质要求的严格程度取决于供水的用途。"

②句中 that 引导的表语从句中，谓语 be free 是虚拟语气形式，意为"无……的，免除……的"。

全句意为"但是，较通常的要求是，水中无有害的细菌、化学药品和其他污染物，可供饮用。"

③It is desirable that … 意为"最好是，但愿是"；

that make … unpleasant 是定语从句，修饰 substances。

全句意为"也最好是，水中没有异味和外观讨厌的物质。"

④hard water 硬水；exchange … for … 把……换成……；

interfere with 影响，妨碍。

全句意为"有时，硬水还要用钠盐交换溶解的钙、镁盐来加以软化，钠盐对肥皂的作用没有干扰。"

⑤much the same … as 与……几乎相同，大致相同；meet 满足。

as 引出的是定语从句，as 在从句中作状语，从句省略了与主句相同的谓语。

全句意为"用于诸如灌溉和消防目的的供水系统，虽然其操作运行方式与饮用水供水系统的方式大体相同，但水不必满足那样高的净化标准要求。"

UNIT SEVEN

Text   Plumbing
——Background and Status

[1]   One of most important systems developed to protect the health of man and to provide man with a better way of life has been the system of plumbing, which is the piping of potable water to its ultimate use and the draining away of waste materials to a variety of treatment processes.① It is essential in our modern society to recognize that plumbing is to society what② the circulatory system is to man. It is a system which must function efficiently to avoid outbreaks of epidemics and to avoid chemical pollution. Good health practices require that plumbing in a community be free of crossconnections, backflow connections, submerged inlets and poor venting. It also must transport a good quality of potable water in adequate quantities in order to service our modern society. One of the great difficulties that we face as a society is that older existing plumbing may deteriorate and may create health hazards; also, repairs of plumbing may be carried out in such a way that they will create direct health hazards.

[2]   Plumbing is the practice, materials, and fixtures used in installing, maintaining, and altering of pipes, appliances, and appurtenances, utilized for potable water supply, sanitary or storm drainage and venting systems.③ Plumbing does not include the drilling of water wells, installing water softening equipment, or sale of the manufacture or plumbing fixtures, appliances, equipment or hardware. Plumbing systems consist of an adequate potable water supply system, a safe adequate drainage system and ample fixtures and equipment.

[3]   Public health personnel have long been concerned with cross-connections, backflow connections and submerged inlets in plumbing systems and public drinking water supply distribution systems. These cross-connections make possible the contamination of potable water with nonpotable water or contaminated water. Although the probability of contamination of drinking water seems to be remote, a multitude of problems definitely exist. The only proper precaution is to eliminate all the possible links and channels where potable water may be polluted. Cross-connections exist when the individual installing the plumbing is not aware of the danger and may not realize that water can reverse its direction. In fact it may even go uphill. In addition, the valves may fail or may be carelessly left open. In order to combat this problem, installers must understand the hydraulic and pollution factors which can cause environmental health hazards. They must also know what types of standard backflow prevention devices and methods are utilized and how to obtain the materials and install them properly.

[4]   This text on plumbing is not meant to be an overall plumbing guide. It is not even meant to list all of the potential hazards. However, it should provide sufficient material and diagrams to help the environmental health practitioner have a better understanding of plumbing and its effects on health.

[5]　　The current status of the plumbing problem is very difficult to ascertain since data is lacking in this area. However, it can be assumed that plumbing systems in many areas are rapidly deteriorating because of the age of the structures. Unfortunately, about the only new thing added to plumbing in the last 75 years has been the introduction of plastic pipes. As a result of this lack of change, many individuals fail to pay adequate attention to the enormous potential hazard of disease and injury due to microbiological, chemical or physical agents.

New Words and Expressions

plumbing ['plʌmiŋ]	n.	（自来水，卫生）管道（装置）室内给排水系统（管道、工程）
system of plumbing		卫生工程系统（体系）
status ['steitəs]	n.	情形，状况
circulatory ['sɔkjuleitəri]	a.	循环的，流通的
outbreak ['autbreik]	n.	爆发，破裂
epidemic [epi'demik]	n.	流行病，时疫
cross-connection [krɔs-kə'nekʃən]	n.	交叉连接（可能使饮用水污染的连接）
submerged [səb'mə:dʒid]		水面下的
inlet ['inlet]	n.	进（气、水）口
submerged inlet		淹没式入口，进水口淹没
vent [vent]	n.; vt.	通风（排气）管（口）；排出，放气
service ['sə:vis]	vt.; n.	服（勤、业）务；设备（施）（自来水）供给，供水管
deteriorate [di'tiəriəreit]	v.	变质，损坏
appurtenance [ə'pə:tinəns]	n.	（常用复数）附属物，设备；配件；附属建筑（装置）
sanitary or storm drainage		生活用水或雨水的排放
distribution [distri'bju:ʃən]	n.	分布，配给
multitude ['mʌltitju:d]	n.	许多，大批（量）
a multitude of		许多的，众多的
uphill ['ʌp'hil]	n.; a.; ad.	上坡，向上
valve [vælv]	n.	阀门，开关
combat ['kɔmbət]	v.	和……作斗争，反对

Notes

① 这是一个复合句。句中 "developed to protect … and to provide …and to provide way of life" 是过去分词短语, 作后置定语, 修饰 "systems", "to protect … " 是并列的不定式短语, 作目的状语, "which" 引导的是非限制性定语从句, 修饰 "system of plumbing"。

② "what" 在此句中起连接词 "as" 的作用, 意为 "正如（犹如）", 引出方式状语从句。

③ 这一句虽然偏长, 但却是简单句。句中 "used in … and venting systems" 是过去分词短语, 作后置定语, 修饰 "practice, materials and fixtures"; 其中 "utilized for … systems" 作 "pipes, appliances, appurtenances" 的后置定语。

Exercises

Reading Comprehension

Ⅰ. Say whether the following statements are True (T) or False (F) according to the text.

1. Good health practices do not require that plumbing in a community be free of cross connections, backflow connections, submerged inlets and poor venting. (   )
2. It also must transport a good quality of potable water in adequate quantities in order to service our modern society. (   )
3. Plumbing includes the drilling of water wells, installing water softening equipment, or the manufacture or sale of plumbing fixtures, appliances, equipment or hardware. (   )
4. Plumbing systems consist of an adequate potable water supply system, a safe adequate drainage system and ample fixtures and equipment. (   )
5. The current status of the plumbing problem is not very difficult to ascertain, although data is lacking in this area. (   )
6. Cross-connections exist when the individual installing the plumbing is aware of the danger and may realize that water can reverse its direction. (   )
7. One of the great difficulties that we face as a society is not that older existing plumbing may deteriorate. (   )
8. It can be assumed that plumbing systems in many areas are rapidly deteriorating plumbing because of the age of the structures. (   )
9. This text on plumbing is meant to be an overall plumbing guide. (   )
10. Cross-connections do not make possible the contamination of potable water with non-potable water or contaminated water. (   )

Ⅱ. Identify main ideas for each paragraph by matching the following ideas with their appropriate paragraph numbers.

A. Plumbing systems in many areas are rapidly deteriorating because of   (1)
   the age of the structures.
B. Plumbing systems are composed of an adequate potable water system,   (3)
   a safe adequate drainage system, and ample fixtures and equipment.
C. The system of plumbing is the piping of potable water to its ultimate use (4)
   and the drainage away of waste materials to a variety of treatment processes.
D. This passage on plumbing is not meant to be an overall plumbing guide.   (2)
E. Public health personnel have long been concerned with cross-connections, (5)
   backflow connections and submerged inlets in plumbing systems and public
   drinking water supply distribution systems.

Vocabulary

I. Fill in the blanks with the verbs given below, change the forms if necessary.

| protect | function | include | maintain | avoid |
| circulate | exist | utilize | combat | alter |

1. While _____ in the ground, on the surface of the earth or even in the air, water becomes polluted.
2. To _____ a consistent relationship between atoms, chemists, use quantities termed moles.
3. Whatever source of water is _____ ——lakes, rivers, springs or wells——the available supply depends on the nature and the size of the catchment, and the amount of rain that falls thereon.
4. The coating _____ the metal from attack by oxygen, the real corrosive agent.
5. A person dies when his brain ceases to _____.
6. Because of the large number of different kinds of impurities, water needs treating before use in order to make it suitable for its intended applications or after use in order to _____ harming the environment.
7. You will find the plan _____ most of your suggestions.
8. Nothing can _____ the fact that our earth has been polluted.
9. There are several ways in which water pollution can be _____.
10. One cannot _____ without water.

II. Complete each of the following statements with one of the four choices given below.
1. In the plumbing fixtures undue noise should be _____.
   A. included   B. eliminated   C. got   D. taken
2. All gases and unwanted odors must be _____ to the outdoor air.
   A. make   B. put   C. vented   D. denied
3. All bathrooms must be properly _____ and ventilated.

      A. lighted   B. decorated   C. beautified   D. tightened

4. Devices used for heating and storing of water must be designed and installed to avoid the danger of _____ or explosion.

      A. overloading   B. overcharging   C. overcrowding   D. overheating

5. Public sewers should be utilized whenever _____.

      A. interesting   B. possible   C. important   D. impossible

Reading Material A

Basic Principles of Plumbing

There are certain basic principles of environmental health and safety that are satisfied through the proper design, installation and maintenance of a good plumbing system. Although the details of plumbing construction may vary, the health of the public must be protected. The following 22 items cover these principles:

1. All occupied premises used for human habitation must have a potable source of water, which is safe and protected against the hazards of backflow or back-siphonage.
2. Water must be provided at all use outlets in the plumbing fixtures at pressures and at quantities which make the system functional for human use. Undue noise should be eliminated.
3. Hot and cold running water is required at all plumbing fixtures which are normally used for washing or cleaning.
4. Water should be utilized in quantities consistent with proper performance and cleaning and yet in compliance with necessary water conservation measures. ①
5. Devices used for heating and storing of water must be designed and installed to avoid the danger of overheating or explosion.
6. Public sewers should be utilized whenever possible.
7. Each family dwelling unit must have at least one sink and stool in a bathroom and a separate sink for the kitchen, as well as a bathtub or shower.
8. The drainage system has to be designed, constructed and maintained in such a way that it will not clog readily, but if it does clog adequate cleanouts will be provided.
9. The piping within the plumbing system must be made of durable material and be free of defects to give a long expected life of service.
10. Each fixture directly connected to the drainage system has to be equipped with a liquid seal cap to trap gases created in the sewer system.
11. The trap seals must be protected in the design of the drainage system by providing adequate circulation of air in all pipes and by eliminating the possibility of siphonage, aspiration or breaking of the trap seals under ordinary use conditions.

12. All gases and unwanted odors must be vented to the outer air.
13. The plumbing system must be put under pressure to test for leaks and defects in the workmanship or material.
14. Materials, that clog or help clog pipes, produce explosive mixtures, destroy the pipes or their joints, or interfere with the sewage disposal process must not be put into the building drainage system.
15. All food, water, and sterile goods must be protected against backflow of sewage or against leaking sewage from overhead pipes.
16. All bathrooms must be properly lighted and ventilated.
17. Where on-site sewage disposal systems are necessary, they must conform to local and state standards and be able to perform under unusual conditions.
18. If a plumbing drainage system is subject to[2] backflow of sewage from the public sewer, adequate protective measures should be used to keep the sewage from entering the building.
19. Plumbing systems must be maintained in a safe and serviceable state.
20. Plumbing fixtures have to be accessible for cleaning and for maintenance.
21. Plumbing must be installed in such a way that the structural members such as walls and floors will not be damaged.
22. Sewage or other waste must not be discharged onto the surface, into storm water drains, or into the subsurface water supply.

Notes

①水的使用量应足以维持设备的正常功能和清洗工作，同时也应符合节约用水的标准。
②subject to 易受……之损害。

Reading Material B

Sources of Water

Rivers

The most direct and readily available source of water is a river. A river is the main artery which transfers water from the catchment areas in the hills to the sea. It is seldom sufficient in itself as a large-scale dependable supply since the volume of water carried in it fluctuates rapidly. However it is a prime source from which water can be abstracted at any point on its course and put into storage. A river may feed a reservoir directly or water may be abstracted from the river and pumped overland to the reservoir. When rivers are used in this way, care must be taken to ensure that there are no harmful effects to downstream river users.

Rivers often transport effluent to the sea. In both the river and the sea, bacteria degrade the organic wastes in the water and purify it, providing there is suffcient dissolved oxygen present. ① To provide enough oxygen for this process a minimum volume of water must be present in the river at all times. The lowest volume of water needed for this is known as the minimum acceptable flow (M. A. F.) or , alternatively, as the compensation water. This may be greater or less than the dry weather flow (D. W. F.) —an alternative method of describing periods of low flow, which as yet has no unique definition. Failure to maintain the M. A. F. may result in anaerobic conditions arising in the river. The end product of degradation under anaerobic condition (this time by types of bacteria that do not need dissolved gaseous oxygen) includes hydrogen sulphide and methane (marsh gas), which are undesirable and unpleasant.

Alternative Sources

An alternative natural source of water is found in wells and springs. Both these sources are related to the groundwater. When rain falls on the land it may flow straight into a river (a process known as runoff) and so becomes quickly available as a water supply. Depending upon the state of the ground (that is, how much water it already contains) a proportion of this precipitation may percolate down into the rocks. Some rocks are more permeable to water than others , Rock strata that will hold water are known as aquifers. An aquifer is usually bounded on the bottom (and sometimes on the top) by an impermeable stratum, so that the water in an aquifer is only available for use by borehole, from a well or when the aquifer reaches the surface (usually on a hillside) to form a spring. ②As a natural water source, groundwater has been in use for centuries. More recently (the last hundred years or so) groundwater has also been added to the list of artificially maintained sources, water is removed from the aquifer by pumping ——a natural or artesian well needs no pumping when the head of water is sufficient. As the level of groundwater (often referred to as the water table) falls, more pumping is necessary. During times of heavy rain the aquifer will recharge itself naturally, although this may not be fast enough to satisfy the pumping rate indefinitely. In this case it is necessary (and economically viable) to pump excess water back into the aquifer to replenish it.

The use of ground water from aquifers is limited by the number of suitable strata that are available. Aquifers represent underground storage and as such can be regarded as subterranean reservoirs. They occupy no land surface and so no valuable agricultural or building land is lost. The water contained in them is purer since it is less open to atmospheric pollution. However this fact in itself may sometimes be a severe handicap. Unlike rivers, where the passage of water from the hills to the sea can be measured in days or weeks, the time taken by groundwater for the same journey an be years or centuries. If any pollutant is accidentally introduced into the groundwater, then its removal by natural flushing is a very long procedure.

Notes

① …providing there is sufficient dissolved oxygen present.

……只要水中有足够的溶解氧。

② 含水层常以底部（有时是顶部）的不透水层为界，所以含水层的水只能用钻孔的方法，或者从井中，或者含水层在地面露头（通常在山边）而形成泉时，才可以取用。

UNIT EIGHT

Text   Microbes as Chemical Machines

[1]   In 1857 Louis Pasteur published a report showing that the souring of milk is caused by microbes which convert milk sugar into lactic acid. The process can be chemically expressed as follows:

$$\underset{\text{(sugar)}}{C_6H_{12}O_6} \longrightarrow \underset{\text{(lactic acid)}}{2CH_3CHOHCOOH}$$

[2]   In its gross result and in appearance at least, this is one of the simplest chemical changes that can be imagined, representing as it does the breakdown of one molecule of sugar into two molecules of lactic acid.

[3]   Let us now turn to another transformation of sugar studied by Pasteur during the same period, namely alcoholic fermentation as exemplified by the conversion of grape juice into wine In this case, as is well known, the microorganism responsible for the change is yeast, which converts the sugar of grape juice into alcohol according to the following equation.

$$\underset{\text{(sugar)}}{C_6H_{12}O_6} \longrightarrow \underset{\text{(alcohol)}}{2CH_3CH_2OH} + 2CO_2$$

The Presence or Absence of Oxygen

[4]   When left exposed to the air,[①] wine will turn into vinegar, and this is precisely the next problem to which Pasteur addressed himself. He showed that in this case the change is caused by still another type of microorganism, which oxidizes alcohol into acetic acid according to the following formula:

$$\underset{\text{(alcohol)}}{CH_3CH_2OH} + O_2 \longrightarrow \underset{\text{(acetic acid)}}{CH_3COOH} + H_2O$$

[5]   As we have just seen, the conversion of sugar into lactic acid or alcohol occurs independently of the presence of oxygen, whereas the conversion of alcohol into acetic acid results from an oxidation in which atmospheric oxygen participates. In contrast, Pasteur observed that when a sugar solution was placed in an atmosphere from which the oxygen had been completely removed a very different kind of substance was likely to appear, namely butyric acid. Under these conditions, the bacteria which proliferate live best without oxygen and in fact may die in the presence of this gas. "Anaerobic" bacteria (to use an expression suggested by Pasteur himself) convert sugar into butyric acid according to the following general formula, which corresponds to "anaerobic" fermentation, that is, one not involving the use of oxygen.

$$\underset{\text{(sugar)}}{C_6H_{12}O_6} \longrightarrow \underset{\text{(butyric acid)}}{CH_3CH_2CH_2COOH}$$

The World of Microbes

[6]   I have listed four different types of chemical processes, not only to demonstrate the range of Pasteur's contributions to microbial chemistry, but even more to illustrate the chemical versatility of microorganisms. The important lesson to be learned from these simple examples is that given a certain substance,② it can be transformed into many different derivative substances depending upon the types of microbes to which it is exposed, and upon the particular conditions under which microbial action takes place.

[7]   Pasteur discovered that each type of microbe is more or less specialized in a few chemical reactions; and for every kind of organic substance there exists in nature at least one and usually several kinds of microbes capable of attacking and breaking down this substance provided the conditions are right. The many types of microorganisms that are present almost everywhere in nature break down all complex organic substances step by step into simpler and simpler chemical compounds. They are necessary links in the endless chain which binds life to matter and matter to life. Without them life would soon come to an end.

[8]   Further evidence of the immense part that microorganisms play in the world of nature is found in the fact that, according to recent calculations, the total mass of microbial life on earth is approximately twenty times greater than the total mass of animal life!

[9]   During recent decades scientists working on microbial nutrition have found that vitamins provide still further evidence of similarity among the different forms of life——from the largest to the smallest. It must be said in truth that many microorganisms can grow in culture media lacking sufficient vitamin for the survival and growth of animals and men. But the reason is that these microorganisms can themselves synthesize the vitamins from simpler materials and thus produce enough to satisfy their own needs. In other words, whether microorganisms do or do not require preformed vitamins for growth, they utilize these substances for their biochemical activities in much the same way as do plants, animals, and men. ③

New Words and Expressions

microbe ['maikrəub]	n.	微生物，细菌
lactic ['læktik]	a.	乳的
lactic acid		乳酸
as it does		实际上
breakdown ['breikdaun]	n.	分解，离解
fermentation [fə;men'teiʃən]	n.	发酵
exemplify [ig'zemplifai]	vt.	举例说明，作为……的例子
equation [i'kweiʃən]	n.	反应式，公式
address oneself to…		论述，谈到

oxidize [ˈɔksidaiz]	v.	使氧化
acetic [əˈsiːtik]	a.	醋（乙）酸的
acetic acid		醋（乙）酸
independently of		与……无关，不取决于
oxidation [ɔksiˈdeiʃən]	n.	氧化（作用）
atmospheric [ætməsˈferik]	a.	大气（中）的，空气的
butyric [ˈbjuːtirik]	a.	丁酸的，奶油的
butyric acid		丁酸
bacteria [bækˈtiəriə]	n.	(bacterium 的复数) 细菌
proliferate [prəuˈlifəreit]	v.	繁殖，繁衍
anaerobic [æneiəˈrəubik]	a.	厌氧的，厌气的
versatility [vəːsəˈtiliti]	n.	多面性，多功能性
derivative [diˈrivətiv]	a.	转生的，派生的，衍生的
specialize [ˈspeʃəlaiz]	v.	使专门化，特殊化
attack [əˈtæk]	vt.	（化学）腐蚀，锈蚀
step by step		逐步，逐渐
calculation [kælkjuˈleiʃən]	n.	计算，统计
nutrition [njuː(ː)ˈtriʃən]	n.	营养（学）
in truth		实际上，说实在话
culture [ˈkʌltʃə]	n.	培养，养殖
media [ˈmiːdiə]	n.	(medium 的复数) 培养基
culture media		培养基
synthesize [ˈsinθisaiz]	v.	（人工）合成
preform [ˈpriːfɔːm]	vt.	预先形成
biochemical [ˈbaiəuˈkemikəl]	a.	生物化学的

Notes

①状语从句 When left exposed to the air 中有省略现象，完整的句子为 When wine is left exposed to the air；exposed to the air 为过去分词短语充当被省略的主语的 wine 的补足语。

②given a certain substance 为过去分词引起的短语作状语。

③连词 as 引导的定语从句中出现主谓倒装结构，正常的顺序为 as plants, animals and men do.

Exercises

Reading Comprehension

I. Say whether the following statements are true (T) or False (F) according to the text.
1. The souring of milk is caused by microbes which break down one molecule of sugar into two molecules of lactic acid. ( )
2. The conversion of grape juice into wine is caused by yeast, which oxidizes alcohol into acetic acid. ( )
3. Wine will turn into vinegar in an atmosphere from which oxygen is completely removed. ( )
4. The conversion of sugar into lactic acid occurs independently of the presence of oxygen, but this is not the case in the conversion of sugar into alcohol. ( )
5. Pasteur discovered that butyric acid was likely to appear when a sugar solution was placed in an atmosphere without oxygen. ( )
6. Anaerobic bacteria live best without oxygen and may die in the presence of this gas. ( )
7. Some organic substances cannot be broken down by microbes even if the conditions are right. ( )
8. It has been found that the total mass of microbial life on earth is almost as much as the total mass of animal life. ( )
9. Few microorganisms can grow in culture media lacking sufficient vitamin for the survival and growth of animals and men. ( )
10. Many microorganisms can utilize simpler materials for their biochemical activities without preformed vitamins. ( )

II. Identify main ideas for each paragraph by matching the following ideas with their appropriate paragraph numbers.

A. Many microorganisms can themselves synthesize the vitamins (7)
  from simpler materials and thus produce enough to satisfy their own needs.
B. The conversion of sugar into butyric acid is caused by anaerobic (3)
  bacteria, which live best in an atmosphere without oxygen and may die
  in the presence of this gas
C. The many types of microorganisms existing almost everywhere in (6)
  nature break down all complex organic substances into simpler and simpler
  chemical compounds.
D. The microorganism responsible for the conversion of grape (9)
  juice into wine is yeast, which converts sugar into alcohol.
E. Microorganisms are chemically versatile. (5)

Vocabulary

I. Fill in the blanks with the verbs given below, change the form if necessary.

| require | specialize | proliferate | represent | attack |
| synthesize | demonstrate | exemplify | convert | involve |

1. It has been _____ that the use of ozone in the treatment of water with high humic content, increases microbial growth in the distribution system.
2. The environment must also furnish sufficient energy to permit the bacteria to _____ the protoplasm.
3. Naturally occurring bacteria which digest and _____ harmful pollutants are released in quantity at the site of the pollution.
4. The bacteriological analysis of drinking water _____ culturing coliform bacteria in a selective growth media and controlled environment.
5. The plant is producing around 1.4 million gallons of water a day, which _____ around 40% of the island's current consumption.
6. Careful control of contamination in museums and galleries _____ strict monitoring, and the use of the most appropriate materials.
7. The act _____ the political interaction of state and local governments that become necessary to provide workable public water systems using public funds.
8. Those types of fish that do survive find that food is plentiful and they often _____.
9. The strong acid _____ the metal cup so that there appeared a small hole in it.
10. _____ bacterial strains have the ability to utilize dissolved H_2S in their metabolic process.

II. Complete each of the following statements with one of the four choices given below.
1. Bacteria obtain their energy either from sunlight or from _____ of chemical compounds.
   A. fermentation B. microorganism C. yeast D. oxidation
2. _____ streams are recognized by floating sludge solids and the formation of gas which bubbles to the surface.
   A. Lactic B. Acetic C. Butyric D. Anaerobic
3. The bacteria _____ the pollutants till they slowly settle out as fine sludge.
   A. break down B. correspond to C. transform into D. depend on
4. Several innovative design features are incorporated to increase user _____ and convenience.
   A. nutrition B. similarity C. versatility D. calculation
5. Heavy _____ pollution occurs in most of the larger towns in this country, with consequent detriment to health and environment.

A. biochemical	B. atmospheric	C. derivative	D. microbial

Reading Material A

Bacteria

The basic group of microorganisms of importance to the sanitary engineer are the bacteria. These microorganisms are the cause of most sanitary problems. Uncontrolled, the bacteria produce odors and objectionable conditions. Some bacteria attack higher plants and animals and destroy them. It is the sanitary engineer's job to see that the pathogenic bacteria are destroyed before they do damage. He also uses the bacteria under controlled conditions in waste treatment plants to stabilize organic matter and thereby prevent objectionable conditions.

bacteria are the basic plant unit, being the simplest form of plant life. Many people find it difficult to believe that bacteria are plants and not animals. This erroneous impression is derived from the fact that plant life is associated with photosynthesis and the presence of green pigment, chlorophyll. Most bacteria, especially the ones commonly found in nature, do not contain chlorophyll and are colorless. Bacteria are classified as plants because of their structure and method of food intake. They are single-cell organisms which utilize soluble food. Each cell is an independent organism capable of carrying out all the necessary functions of life.

Distribution

Bacteria are found everywhere in nature: in water, in soil, and in air. Most of the bacteria are found in water and in soil which has a high moisture content, for the bacteria must have an aqueous environment to obtain food. The bacteria in the air are associated largely with particulate materials. Bacteria are distributed in nature according to the presence of nutrient materials used as food. Soil contains all types of bacteria necessary for the degradation of organic matter. If bacteria are needed to stabilize unusual organic compounds, the engineer has only to look under his feet to find them.

Metabolism

Metabolism determines the bacteria's ability to grow in any environment. Not only must the environment supply the chemical elements to produce the protoplasm for new cells but it must also furnish sufficient energy to permit the bacteria to synthesize the protoplasm. Bacteria obtain their energy either from sunlight or from oxidation of chemical compounds.

Photosynthesis

A few bacteria utilize the energy from sunlight to synthesize protoplasm. The energy from sunlight is converted by photosynthesizing pigments similar to chlorophyll found in higher plants. The use of energy from sunlight permits the bacteria to utilize carbon dioxide as their source of carbon for protoplasm. The mechanism of carbon dioxide fixation by photosynthetic bacteria differs from that of higher plants in that oxygen is not evolved.① The basic equations for photosynthesis by bacteria and higher plants are shown in Eqs. (4-1) and (4-2).

Higher Plants

$$XCO_2 + NH_3 + ZH_2O \xrightarrow{\text{Sunlight}} C_xH_yO_zN + XO_2 \tag{4-1}$$

Bacteria

$$XCO_2 + NH_3 + \frac{X}{2}H_2S + ZH_2O \xrightarrow{\text{Sunlight}} C_xH_yO_zN + \frac{X}{2}H_2SO_4 \tag{4-2}$$

Basically, the two equations are similar, with the exception that the bacterial photosynthesis reaction oxidizes hydrogen sulfide rather than releasing free oxygen.② There is some evidence that the blue-green algae will react in the same manner as the photosynthetic bacteria if hydrogen sulfide is present. Very little is known about these bacteria and they are of little importance to sanitary microbiologists other than to know that photosynthetic bacteria do exist.③

Chemosynthesis

The oxidation of inorganic or organic compounds to obtain energy for synthesis is called chemosynthesis and is the most common method of bacterial metabolism. The bacteria which oxidize inorganic compounds utilize carbon dioxide for their protoplasm and are called autotrophic bacteria. The bacteria which oxidize organic compounds for energy obtain the carbon for synthesis from the same organic compound used for energy.④ A portion of the organic compound is used for energy and a portion is used for synthesis. These bacteria are known as heterotrophic. Both the autotrophic and the heterotrophic bacteria are important to sanitary microbiology.

Notes

①二氧化碳被光能合成细菌固定的机理与高等植物固定二氧化碳的机理的不同之处就在于不释放氧气。
②这两个反应式基本相似，但除去一点，即细菌的光能合成反应使硫化氢氧化，而非释放游离氧。
③人们对这些细菌知之甚少，且它们对于卫生微生物学家来说也无关紧要，而重要的是要知道光能合成细菌确实存在。
④对有机化合物进行氧化而获取能量的细菌能从该有机化合物中获得合成所需的碳。

Reading Material B

Water Pollution and Its Effect on Environment

Water pollution occurs due to the presence of dissolved inorganic materials, organic materials such as proteins, fat, carbonhydrates and other substances found in domestic and industrial waters, and physical factors such as turbidity, colour, temperature of effluent, associated radioactivity, etc. ①

The industrial wastes from the factories that use water are probably a greatest single water pollution problem. In most cases the organic wastes, as potent as they might be,② are at least treatable in or out of the plant. Inorganic industrial wastes are much trick to control and potentially more hazardous. Chromium from metal-plating plants is an old source of trouble, but mercury discharges have only recently received their due attention. As important as these and other well-known "heavy metals" might be, many scientists are much more concerned with unknown chemicals. Industy is creating a fantastic array of new chemicals each year, all of which eventually find their way to the water. For most of these, not even the chemical formulas are known, much less their acute, chronic or genetic toxicity. ③

Municipal waste is a source of water pollution second in importance only to industrial wastes. Around the turn of the century, most discharges from municipalities received no treatment whatsoever. In the United States, sewage from 24 million people was flowing directly into our water courses. Since that time, the population has increased, and so has the contribution from municipal discharges. Even with the billions of dollars spent on building wastewater treatment plants, the contribution from municipal pollution sources has not been significantly reduced. We seem to be holding our own, however, and at least are not falling further behind. ④

In addition to industrial and municipal wastes, water pollution emanates from land erosion, petroleum compounds etc.

It should be amply clear, therefore, that water can be polluted by many types of waste products.

When a high-energy organic material such as raw sewage is discharged to a stream, a number of changes occur downstream from the point of discharge. As the organics are decomposed, oxygen is used at a greater rate than before the pollution occurred, and the dissolved oxygen (DO) level drops. The rate of reaeration, or solution of oxygen from the air, also increase, but this is often not great enough to prevent a total depletion of oxygen in the streams. When this happens, the stream is said to become anaerobic. An anaerobic stream is easily identifiable. Since oxygen is no longer around to act as the hydrogen acceptor, ammonia and hydrogen sulfide are formed, among other gases. ⑤ Some of these gases will dissolve readily, but others will attach themselves as bubbles to hunks of black solid material, known as benthic deposits (or simply sludge), and buoy this material to the surface. Anaerobic streams are thus recognized by floating sludge solids and the formation of gas which bubbles to the surface.

It is logical to assume that such outward changes can also be described by the effect on aquatic life. Indeed, the increased turbidity, settled solid matter and low DO all contribute to a decrease in fish life. Fewer and fewer species of fish are able to survive, but those types of fish that do survive find that food is plentiful and they often multiply in numbers.

It is important to remember that the reactions of stream to pollution outlined above occur when a rapidly decomposable organic material is wasted. The stream will react much differently to inorganic wastes, say from a metal-plating plant. ⑥ If the waste is toxic to aquatic life, both the kind and total number of organisms will decrease. The DO will not fall, and might even rise. There are many types of pollution, and a stream will react differently to each. Even more complicated is a situation where two or more wastes are involved.

Notes

① 水污染的发生是由于水中存在的溶解的无机物，有机物（如蛋白质，脂肪，碳水化合物），生活及工业用水中的其它物质，以及象废水的浊度，温度，有关的放射性等物理因素而引起的。

② …, as potent as they might be, …
……，尽管它们污染性很强，……

③ 对大多数这些新的化学物质，人们甚至连其化学分子式都不知道，更不用说它们急性的，慢性的或遗传性的毒性了。

④ 然而我们似乎正维持现状，至少没有让污染进一步恶化。

⑤ 因为已没有氧来充当氢的接受体，硫化氢便连同其它气体一道形成了。

⑥ 对于比方说从金属电镀厂排出的无机废物，河流所作出的反应将大为不同。

UNIT NINE

Text   Groundwater Formation and Its Movement

[1]   In addition to surface freshwater systems, another important source of industrial, domestic, and agricultural water is groundwater. Recent data indicate that over 81 billion gallons of groundwater per day is used in the continental United States. This represents 20% of all the water used in this country. Of this amount, 42 billion gallons per day is used in agricultural irrigation, 31 billion gallons is used in rural areas, and 8 billion gallons is used for municipal and industrial purposes. The source of this groundwater is that portion of rain or snow that travels below the zone of unsaturated water and enters the groundwater table.

[2]   A portion of the water entering the ground will be trapped by rock, soil, and so on, and remain in the upper soil zone as suspended water. Suspended water is prevented from moving deeper into the soil by the molecular attractions that are exerted on the water by the surrounding soil particles, as well as by the intermolecular attractions exerted by water molecules on each other. Since the spaces between the soil particles in this zone are filled with a mixture of air and water, this portion of the soil is termed the zone of aeration and is subdivided into three distinct horizons: the horizon of soil moisture, the intermediate horizon (which may or may not be present), and the capillary fringe.

[3]   A portion of the water that enters the horizon of soil moisture may be either evaporated or transpired. The remainder passes into the intermediate horizon, where it tends to be held as suspended water by molecular attractions. There is little water movement in the intermediate horizon, except during periods of precipitation, when additional incoming water enters this horizon. In some areas the intermediate horizon is absent, and the horizon of soil moisture lies directly over the third horizon-the capillary fringe. Water moves into the capillary fringe (by capillary action) from below.

[4]   The zone of saturation lies below the zone of aeration. In this zone there is no trapped air and the openings in the soil are completely saturated with groundwater. The boundary between the zones of saturation and aeration is termed the water table, which is defined as that point where subsurface water will flow into a well under the force of gravity. The amount, degree of motion, and depth of groundwater is controlled by the structure of the soil and subsoil[①]. Most soils and subsoils are composed of rock and rock fragments that vary in size, density, and compaction. The particles may be small and regular in shape, which results in a close intergranular "fit" with little pore space between the particles[②]. Owing to the low degree of pore space, these subsoils cannot hold much water between the particles and are said to be of low permeability. In other words, subsoils of this nature have little ability to hold or transmit fluids. An example of such a subsoil is clay. Other subsoils may consist of large, irregularly shaped particles that fit together poorly. This type of structure results in many small, inter-

connecting pore spaces into which water may flow and move. Subsoils of this type has a high ability to hold and transmit fluids and is said to be permeable. Subsoils of gravel or sand are highly permeable materials. A recognizable portion of the subsoil that is permeable and through which water moves is termed an aquifer. ③

[5] Below the water table, in the zone of saturation, groundwater tends to flow through the interconnected pore spaces by a process termed percolation. In response to the force of gravity groundwater moves from areas of high water table to areas of low water table. Recharge of groundwater occurs by means of the percolation of rain and melt waters into the soil. Because of the variation in both precipitation and permeability, the percolation rates are not uniform, and this leads to an uneven water table which will tend to be high in areas of high rainfall (or high permeability) and low in areas of low rainfall (or low permeability). This uneven distribution causes groundwater to be in constant motion as it flows under the influence of gravity, from areas of high-water-table level (high hydraulic head) to areas of a lower hydraulic head (low-water-table level). In general, groundwater tends to flow toward surface streams and ponds. The rate of groundwater flow is governed by the permeability of the aquifer and the hydraulic head within the system. The velocity of groundwater is equal to the hydraulic gradient (the differences in water pressure per unit distance) times the coefficient of permeability. This coefficient represents the degree to which the substrate will permit the flow of water. If the velocity is known, the volume of flow (hydraulic conductivity) through the sediment can be calculated. Velocities and direction of groundwater flow are generally determined by introducing dye into recharge wells and monitoring adjacent test wells until the dye travels to these sites. An alternative method, used when dissolved materials interfere with the detection of dye, is adding sodium chloride to the recharge well and monitoring the test well until the chloride ions are detected.

[6] Groundwater movements are slow in comparison with surface waters. Movement in deep aquifers ranges from less than 0.5 centimeter (cm) per day to approximately 100 cm/day. In the majority of aquifers, groundwater moves at rates of only a few centimeters per day, whereas in very permeable soils and subsoils near the surface, velocities may be as high as 15 cm/day.

New Words and Expressions

municipal [mjuːnisipəl]	a.	城市的
unsaturated [ʌnˈsætʃəreitid]	a.	未饱和的
suspended water		悬着水
intermolecular [intəmˈlekjulə]	a.	分子间的
aeration [ɛəˈreiʃən]	n.	曝气，通气
the zone of aeration		通气层
remainder [riˈmeində]	n.	剩余物

capillary *	[kə'piləri]	a.; n.	毛细管（的）
fringe	[frindʒ]	n.	边缘，端
transpire	[træn'spaiə]	v.	蒸发，气化
compaction	[kəm'pækʃən]	n.	压实，压缩
pore	[pɔː]	n.	小孔
intergranular	[intəgræ'njulə]	a.	（颗）粒间的
permeable	['pəːmiəbl]	a.	可渗透的
permeability *	[pəːmiə'biliti]	n.	渗透性，透气性
recognizable	['rekəgnaizəbl]	a.	可认出的
aquifer	['ækwifə]	n.	蓄（含）水层
percolation	[pəkə'leiʃən]	n.	渗透
recharge well			回灌井
hydraulic	[hai'drɔːlik]	a.	水力学的
gradient *	['greidiənt]	n.	梯度，斜度
coefficient *	['kəuifiʃənt]	n.	系数
substrate	['sʌbstreit]	n.	基质，底质
sediment	['sedimənt]	n.	沉积（物）
adjacent *	[ə'dʒeisənt]	a.	邻（靠）近的，相邻的
sodium *	['səudjəm]	n.	钠
sodium chloride			氯化钠
ion	['aiən]	n.	离子

Notes

①The amount, degree of motion, and depth … the soil and subsoil. 一般说来，由 and 连接的两个（或两个以上）名词或代词作主语时，谓语要用复数。但如果表示一个单一概念，谓语则用单数。

②The particles may be …the particles. 句中，which results in a close intergranular "fit" with little pore space between the particles。是由关系代 which 引出的是非限制性定语从句。which 代表整个主句，且为从句的主语，谓语是第三人称单数。

③A recognizable portion …is termed an aquifer。句中 through which water moves is termed an aquifer. 是介词＋关系代词 which 引出的定语从句。

Exercises

Reading Comprehension

Ⅰ. Say whether the following statements are True (T) or (F) according to the text.

1. Recent information points out that more than 81 billion gallons of ground-water per day is used in the United States, this accounts for approximately 30 percent of all the water used. ( )
2. The source of groundwater is that part of rain or snow that runs beneath the zone of saturated water and enters the ground water table. ( )
3. There is little water movement in the intermediate horizon unless additional incoming water enters this horizon during the periods of rain fall. ( )
4. A portion of soil consists of rock and rock fragments that vary in size, weight and compaction. ( )
5. Owing to the low degree of pore space, these subsoils cannot hold much water between the particles and are said to be of low permeability. ( )
6. Since the water table is uneven, it will tend to be high in regions of low permeability. ( )
7. Groundwater usually tends to soak into surface rivers and pore spaces between the soil particles. ( )
8. The velocity of groundwater is equal to the differences in waters pressure per unit distance times the coefficient of permeability. ( )
9. The permeability of the material through which the water flows is accounted for by multiplying the right side of the equation by a proportionality factor. ( )
10. In greater number of aquifers, groundwater moves at rates of only a few cm/day, but its velocity may be as high as 15 cm/day in permeable soils and subsoils. ( )

II. Choose the best answer according to the text.
1. Recent data indicate that _____ is used in agricultural irrigation per day in the U.S..
   A. over 81 billion gallons of groundwater per day
   B. more than 42 billion gallons of groundwater per day
   C. over 31 million gallons of groundwater per day
   D. less than 81 billion gallons of groundwater per day
2. A part of the water entering the ground will be trapped by _____.
   A. saturated layer
   B. ground surface
   C. rock, soil and so on
   D. unsaturated water
3. A recognizable part of the subsoil that is permeable and through which water moves is known as _____.
   A. an aquifer
   B. the capillary fringe
   C. the water table
   D. the zone of aeration
4. The rate of groundwater flow is governed by _____.

A. the permeability of the aquifer and the hydraulic head within the system.
  B. the high hydraulic head
  C. the lower hydraulic head
  D. the force of gravity
5. Velocities and direction of groundwater flow are generally determined by _____ dye into recharge well.
  A. causing   B. changing
  C. throwing   D. flowing

Vocabulary

Ⅰ. Complete the following sentences with some of the words or expressions listed below. Changing the form where necessary.

| compaction | hydraulic | particle | velocity |
| transmit | horizon | attraction | irrigation |

1. Many _____ projects are potentially useful for more than one of the basic purposes.
2. Natural surface waters from streams, lakes, and ponds are used extensively for _____, for industrial purposes, and for city water supplies.
3. In general, solids _____ sound faster than either liquids or gases because solids are more elastic (有弹性).
4. If such a vehicle is moving in deep space with a certain velocity, it will continue to move with the same _____.
5. In response to the _____ of gravity groundwater moves from areas of high water table to areas of low water table.

Ⅱ. Complete each of the following statements with one of the four choices given below.
1. The source of this groundwater is that portion of rain or snow that travels below the zone of _____ and enters the groundwater table.
  A. aeration   B. unsaturated water
  C. natural surface water D. saturated water
2. It is almost impossible to measure how much sewage and industrial waste end up in our oceans, but we can _____ how much oil is discharged into them legally and illegally.
  A. calculate   B. figure
  C. know   D. heard
3. The spaces between the soil _____ in the zone of aeration are full of a mixture of air and water.
  A. molecules   B. clay
  C. particles   D. rocks
4. When pumping liquids, the _____ of the liquid into the pump is generally maintained

by the atmospheric pressure.

A. move   B. form
C. flow   D. kind

5. And molecules are made up of still smaller particles-atoms. Most atoms do not exist singly in nature, but are combined in _____.

A. molecules   B. particles
C. elements   D. atoms

Reading Material A

Sources of Water for Domestic Use

There are three possible sources of water for our daily use. One is rain water collected from roofs of buildings or special water sheds and stored in cisterns or ponds. Another is natural surface water, in streams and lakes. The third and most important in rural areas is ground water stored in the earth's crust.

Rain Water

In regions where there is a fair amount of rainfall, rain water is often collected from building roofs or from outdoor water sheds, and stored in cisterns or ponds. ① In some rural sections of the country cistern water is used for all domestic and farm purposes, including drinking. This is particularly true where ground water is difficult to obtain or, if obtainable, is for any reason unsatisfactory. When cistern water is used for drinking the cistern should be filled only with clean rain water and should be well protected from contamination. To be absolutely safe for drinking, cistern water should be boiled, chlorinated, or otherwise sterilized.

Cistern water is soft water; therefore, in regions where ground water is especially hard, cisterns are frequently used as a source of soft water for the hot-water supply in homes. ②

Farm ponds are an increasingly important source of water for livestock, irrigation, spraying, and fire fighting. When correctly constructed and properly managed they also provide an important source of food fish. They are useful for recreation such as fishing, swimming, boating, and skating.

Natural Surface Waters

Natural surface waters from streams, lakes, and ponds are used extensively for irrigation, for industrial purposes, and for city water supplies. They are also used to some extent for domestic purposes in rural areas. When used for city water supplies or for domestic purposes, surface waters usually must be treated by filtration and chlorination to make them suitable for human consumption. Water so treated is said to be potable, i.e., suitable for drinking.

Ground Water

The principal source of water for domestic uses in rural areas is ground water from springs and wells. Some cities also use ground water from wells. In some regions irrigation water is pumped from wells.

The character of ground water from springs and wells depends upon the nature and condition of the soil and rock through which it passes.③ If it contacts very little soluble material it will be soft water, and because of the filtering action of the soil it may be cleaner and purer than rain water.

Ground-water storage. That portion of the total rainfall which soaks into the earth's crust (approximately one-third) percolates downward into the porous spaces in the soil and rock where it remains, or from which it finds its way out to the surface in some way. The exact behavior at any particular location depends upon the amount of rainfall and the character of the earth's crust through which it percolates.

Notes

① 在雨量充沛的地方，雨水常从建筑物顶或室外雨水棚收集并储存在蓄水池或水塘里。
② 蓄水池的水是软水，因此，在地下水特别硬的地区，蓄水池常作为供应家庭热水的软水水源。
③ 来自泉或井的地下水的特性，取决于地下水流经的土壤和岩石的性质和状况。

Reading Material B

Multi-purpose Hydraulic Projects

Many hydraulic projects are potentially useful for more than one of the basic purposes-water supply, irrigation, hydroelectric power, navigation, flood control, recreation, sanitation, and wildlife conservation. If joint use can be made of facilities so that benefits are increased without a disproportionate increase in cost, the economic justification of the project is greatly improved. This feature was recognized early in the course of man's development of hydraulic projects. Canals to carry navigation around rapids offered an opportunity to develop hydraulic power. In addition to its use for navigation, the canal served to convey water downstream until a point was reached where the canal grade was well above the stream grade.① Here a water wheel was installed, and a portion of the canal flow diverted back to the stream through a mill-race. Early developments of this type were basically the product of expediency - an opportunity offered itself and was accepted. Comprehensive planning of projects for multiple use is a recent concept.

The rapid growth in multi-purpose design is mainly based on the realization that it is imperative that maximum use be made of our resources. The physical elements of a multi-purpose project (dam, spillway, gate, power plant, etc.) differ in no way from those for a single-purpose project. The success which can be obtained in achieving joint use of storage space in a multi-purpose project depends upon the extent to which the various purposes are compatible.② It is helpful, therefore, to review the requirements of the various uses and to consider the ways in which these uses may be coordinated.

Irrigation, navigation, and water supply all require a volume of water which cannot be jointly used, and hence a project combining these functions must provide a clear allocation of storage space to each. Since power development is not a consumptive use, any water released for the other purposes may be used for power. If the power plant can be operated as a baseload plant, its water requirements may fit in well with the relatively uniform releases for other purposes. If it is proposed to use the plant for peaking, it may be necessary to construct an afterbay or reregulating dam downstream to smooth out the fluctuations of the power release. The afterbay storage capacity need be sufficient only to regulate flows for a few days at a time, in the same manner that a distribution reservoir smooths out the load on a pumping plant. A low-head power plant at the reregulating dam may produce a small amount of baseload power. Since the seasonal variations in power demand may not coincide with the requirements of other uses, it is usually necessary to allocate a certain amount of storage for power use or to provide other plants in the system which can pick up the load during the winter months.③

Notes

①除了用于通航外，还利用了渠道把水引向下游，直止渠道纵坡恰好在河道坡度上面的那点为止。
②在多种用途工程中综合使用蓄水库容所能获得的成功的大小取决于将各种用途协调起来的程度。
③由于季节的变化，电力的要求可能与其它用途的需要不一致，通常必须给电力生产分配一定的库容量，或者提供给本系统能在冬季几个月里承担负荷的其它发电站。

UNIT TEN

Text   Open Channel Flow

[1] Open channel flow is the term applied to fluid motion in which a liquid in a conduit has part of its boundary exposed to atmospheric pressure. The conduit may be completely open to the atmosphere, as in natural river beds or artificial canals and channels, or it may be closed, as in drainage and sewerage pipes that are not running full.

[2] Open channel flow is distinguished, on one hand, from pipe flow in which the fluid is completely surrounded by a solid boundary; and, on the other hand, from free jet flow in which the fluid is completely surrounded by the atmosphere. The presence of the solid boundary in pipe flow can sustain a pressure variation along the surface of the pipe, while the presence of a free surface in open channel flow ensures constancy of pressure along the boundary exposed to the atmosphere.

[3] In the case of flow with friction through a constant-area pipe, a pressure difference has to exist to sustain the flow. In the case of flow with friction in an open channel of constant cross section, the effect of gravity——that is, changes in elevation in the channel——sustains the flow through the channel. As contrasted with pipe flow, the cross-sectional area of the flow can change with different flow condition, subject to the confines of the channel. For example, for flow through a rectangular cross section, a change in the depth of the liquid results in a different rectangular cross section.

[4] Just as in pipe flow, the flow may be laminar or turbulent in character, with turbulent flow constituting the most frequent type when the liquid is water.[①] The analysis of open channel flows is important in situations relating to the determination and control of river flow and in establishing design requirements for irrigation canals.

[5] In this chapter we shall treat the various aspects of steady open channel flow; using the techniques and fundamental equations of fluid flow obtained in preceding chapters.

[6] Before proceeding, a few definitions associated with open channel flow will be given. When the cross section of the flow does not vary along the direction of the flow, the flow is called *uniform*. Otherwise it is called *nonuniform* flow, Thus in uniform open channel flow. the liquid depth is constant and the surface of the liquid is parallel to the channel bottom. When the depth of the liquid varies, we have nonuniform open channel flow (also called varied flow). This type of flow occurs when the shape of the channel cross section changes or when the shape of the channel bottom changes. If the depth increases in the downstream direction, the velocity of the flow slows down and we have retarded flow; while for depth decreasing in the downstream direction, we obtain velocity increases and have accelerated flow.

[7] Uniform flow is achieved in any channel that is sufficiently long and that has a constant channel slope and cross section. An example of how uniform flow is established will now be

given. An irrigation canal has a change in slope, as shown if Figure 10-1. Due to the change in the slope of the channel flow, the flow experiences an acceleration because the component of the gravity force along the flow is greater than the shear force along the channel wall retarding the flow. As the flow accelerates, the shear force will increase as a result of the increased velocity until a value of the velocity is reached when the shear force equals the gravity component.② At this condition of equilibrium, the velocity and liquid depth remain constant and the flow becomes uniform open channel flow.

[8]   Nonuuiform flow caused by a change in the slope of the channel floor is illustrated in Figure 10-1. When a barrier, such as spillway, is placed in the path of uniform flow along a sloping channel, we obtain another example of gradually varied flow. The resulting profile of the water surface behind the barrier is called the backwater curve.

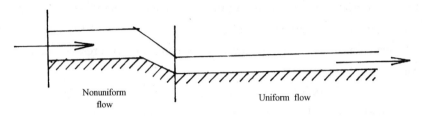

Fig. 10-1   Establishment of uniform channel flow

New Words and Expressions

conduit ['kɔndit]	n.	导管，水管（渠）
sewerage ['sjuəridʒ]	n.	下水道，污水（排水）工程（系统）
constancy ['kɔnstənsi]	n.	（不变，恒定，持久）性
subject ['sʌbdʒikt]	ad.	（与介词 to 连用）受制于，根据，以……为条件
elevation [eli'veiʃən]	n.	高度，海拔
confines ['kɔnfainz]	n. (pl.)	界限，范围，边界
rectangular [rek'tæŋgjulə]	a.	矩（长方）形的
laminar ['læminə]	a.	层（式，状，流）的
turbulent ['tə:bjulənt]	a.	湍（紊）流的
preceding [pri'si:diŋ]	a.	前面的，上述的
～chapters		前几章（上几章）
irrigation [irri'geiʃən]	n.	灌溉（注）
treat [tri:t]	vt.	讨论，论述，探讨
nonuniform ['nɔnju:nifɔ:m]	a.	不均匀的，变化的
～ flow (=varied flow)		变速（不等，紊）流

retard [ri'tɑ:d]	vt.	延迟，减速流
~ed flow		滞流，减速流
component [kəm'pəunənt]	n.	分（力，量，支）
the ~ of the gravity force		重力的分量
shear [ʃiə]	n.	剪（切，力）切（变，力）
~force		切力，剪力
spillway ['spilwei]	n.	溢洪（泄水）道
profile ['prəufail]	n.	轮廓，断面（图）
resulting [ri'zʌltiŋ]	a.	所引起（产生）的
~profile		所形成的剖面图

Notes

① 在这一句中的"with+名词+名词短语"部分相当于冠有"with"的分词独立结构（其中名词与分词短语具有逻辑上的主谓关系），作状语，表示伴随情况。在with引导的短语后面由when引导一个状语从句修饰前面的constituting。

② "As the flow accelerates,…the gravity component."是主从复合句。"As the flow accelerates,"是状语从句，"the shear force will increase as a result of … component,"是主句，其中"as a result of the increased velocity"作状语；"until"又引导一个主从复合句，"a value of velocity is reached"是主句，"when the shear force equals the gravity component"是状语从句。

Exercises

Reading Comprehension

Ⅰ. Say whether the following statements are True (T) or False (F) according to the text.
1. Open channel flow is different from pipe flow in which the fluid is completely surrounded by a solid boundary.   (   )
2. The absence of a free surface in open channel flow ensures constancy of pressure along the boundary exposed to the atmosphere.   (   )
3. The presence of the soft boundary in pipe flow can sustain a pressure variation along the surface of the pipe.   (   )
4. An irrigation canal usually has a change in slope.   (   )
5. When the cross section of the flow varies along the direction of the flow, the flow is called uniform.   (   )
6. When the depth of the liquid varies, nonuniform open channel flow occurs.   (   )
7. In the case of flow without friction through a constant area pipe, a pressure difference

has to exist to sustain the flow. ( )
8. As contrasted with pipe flow, the cross sectional area of the flow can not change with different flow condition, subject to the confines of the channel. ( )
9. The analysis of open channel flows is important in situations relating to the determination and control of river flow and in establishing design requirements for irrigation channels. ( )
10. The resulting profile of the water surface before the barrier is called the backwater curve. ( )

II. Identify the main idea for each paragraph by matching the following ideas with their appropriate paragraph numbers.

    A. How is uniform flow achieved? (1)
    B. Open channel flow is not only distinguished from pipe flow, (4)
    C. What are uniform and nonuniform flow? (2)
    D. What is open channel flow? (6)
    E. The analysis of open channel flows is important. (7)

Vocabulary

I. Fill in the blanks with the verbs given below, change the form if necessary.

achieve	control	distinguish	contrast	expose
surround	relate	remain	retard	sustain

1. Our earth is completely _____ by the atmosphere.
2. If the depth increases in the downstream direction, the velocity of the flow slows down and we have _____ flow.
3. Uniform flow is _____ in any channel that is sufficiently long and that has a constant channel slope and cross section.
4. The presence of the solid boundary in pipe flow can _____ a pressure variation along the surface of the pipe.
5. Large modern dams are constructed across rivers to store and _____ vast quantities of water.
6. The analysis of open channel flows is important in situations _____ to determination and control of river flow and in establishing design requirements for irrigation canals.
7. The presence of a free surface in open channel flow ensures constancy of pressure along the boundary _____ to the atmosphere.
8. We should _____ open channel flow with pipe flow.
9. We should _____ between gross use and consumptive use.
10. At the condition of equilibrium, the velocity and liquid depth _____ constant and the flow becomes uniform open channel flow.

II. Complete each of the following statements with one of the four choices given below.
1. Nonuniform flow caused by a change in the slope of the channel floor is _____ in Figure 10-1.
   A. illustrated   B. made   C. taken   D. got
2. Before proceeding, a few definitions _____ with open channel flow will be given.
   A. compared   B. dealt   C. associated   D. supplied
3. In this chapter we shall _____ the various aspects of steady open channel flow.
   A. obtain   B. gain   C. sustain   D. treat
4. Thus in uniform open channel flow, the liquid depth is constant and the surface of the liquid is _____ to the channel bottom.
   A. equal   B. parallel   C. parallelism   D. paralleled
5. An example of how uniform flow is _____ will now be given.
   A. established   B. distinguished C. accomplished D. published

Reading Material A

Dam

Large modern dams are constructed across rivers to store and control vast quantities of water. And it can be used for irrigation, electric power generation, flood control, navigation, public water supplies, industrial water supplies, and recreation. Some dams serve only one or a few of these purposes, but most modern dams serve several and therefore are called multipurpose dams.

Based on data from more than 61 countries, the World Register of Dams for dams higher than 50 feet shows there are more than 10 000 dams in the world, and more than 250 dams are being added annually worldwide. The United States builds about 100 dams a year that are taller than 50 feet; Japan builds about 30 such dams annually; and India, Italy and Spain each build about 10 such dams annually. During 1963-1965, the USSR[①] built 12 such dams, for an average of 4 dams annually.

In recent times, the demands on water resources caused by expanding populations and economies have increased the need to build dams for water storage.[②] In the United States, for water diverted into waterworks structures, the average water consumption per capita was 137 gallons per day in the late 1960's. This figure includes residential, commercial, and industrial use of water in a community. In towns where there are large industrial users of water, the water requirement per capita is even higher because, for example, it takes 65 000 gallons of water to make a ton of steel and 10 gallons of water to refine a gallon of gasoline.

Although dam building is a key means for controlling and using water resources for the benefit of mankind, it sometimes presents problems because a dam blocks the river, and impedes navigation by vessels and migration by fish. Where a channel for river vessels is required, navigation locks are built alongside the dam. Where fish migration is important, fish locks similar to locks for vessels are provided.③ Fish ladders also are built so that valuable fish, can swim around a dam, The fish enter at the lowest of a series of ascending pools and leap from pool to pool until they get to the reservoir level.

An advanced technology is needed in building a large dam and its related facilities so that they will be economical, useful, and safe from failure. Aerial photographs often are used in the preliminary stages of exploration to locate major geological features at a site. Expert knowledge of hydrology, geology, hydraulics, and other sciences is applied to solve the complex problems encountered in analyzing the foundation rock and soil, laying bare the riverbed at the damsite, and designing and constructing the dam and related facilities. Each material, such as earth, rock, or concrete, to be used in building the dam is selected to produce the desired results in the most economical way at a particular site. Careful analysis and study of each material are made to ensure that the dam will be impervious to water and will be heavy and strong enough to resist the reservoir water pressure against the face of the dam. In high dams, this pressure is tremendous; at the base of the Hoover Dam, for example, the water exerts a pressure of 45 000 psi.

Since ancient times, man has built dams made of earth, rock fill or big stones-materials that have always been readily available. As engineers learned more about these and other materials, they began to build dams of various sizes, shapes, and materials. There are now five principal types: earth dams, rock-fill dams, gravity dams, arch dams, and buttress dams.

Notes

①USSR＝Union of Soviet Socialist Republics 前"苏维埃社会主义共和国联盟"的缩写。
②在近代，由于人口和经济的不断增长，引起了对水源的需要，从而增加了修建储水水坝的要求。
③在鱼类回游很重要的地方，要提供类似于船闸之类的鱼闸。

Reading Material B

Rock-fill Dams and Spillway

Rock-Fill Dams.

A rock-fill dam is formed of loose rock and boulders piled up at a site where there is a solid foundation. In areas where earth is scarce but rock is plentiful, such as sites on streams in mountain regions, dams are formed entirely of broken rock. The rock must be strong enough so that it will not disintegrate during long exposure to weather or moisture, and will not split under the heavy loads to which it would be subjected. ①

Because a rock embankment permits water to pass through it, the dam must be built either with a watertight facing or an impermeable clay, concrete, or rolled-earth core. The watertight facing can be a concrete slab forming the upstream face, or the face can be made of asphaltic cement. A cut-off, or seal, must be built at the bottom of the impervious core or facing to prevent leakage directly underneath the dam.

Some rock-fill dams have been built by using huge rocks, weighing 10 to 15 tons each, and smaller stones to fill the voids. In recent practice, smaller, graded sizes of rock are used, and the rocks are compacted in a way similar to the way that earth is compacted in building earth dams. The slope of a rock-fill dam can be made much steeper than that of an earth dam because of the greater weight and strength of rock. Generally, the face of a rock-fill dam is inclined at an angle of about 36°.

Rock-fill dams are less common than earth dams or concrete dams, but there are a considerable number of them in the United States. An example of a rock-fill dam is Montgomery Dam (1957) in Colorado. It is 113 feet (34 meters) high and has an asphaltic cement upstream face.

Spillway

Although it is desirable to store all inflows to a reservoir so that the water can be put to use, a modern dam generally is provided with a spillway of suitable capacity to release excess water or floodwater. Floodwaters occur only rarely at a damsite, but the spillway is designed to pass the floodwaters and thus minimize the danger of damage or failure to the dam. The spillway is either built as a part of the dam or as a separate structure nearby. The alternative of building the dam high enough to provide for even the most rare flood condition is usually more expensive than building a spillway. ②

A dam can have one of several types of spillways. An overflow spillway is built at a level slightly lower than the crest. A chute spillway is built around the end of a dam. A shaft spillway, called a "glory hole" because it resembles the flower of a morning glory, is built in the reservoir area. As the reservoir rises to the level of the glory hole, the water spills into it and then passes through a lined tunnel to the river below the dam. A gate-controlled spillway has a mechanically operated gate that can be opened when excess water needs to be passed.

It is particularly important that an embankment dam have a spillway capable of discharging the calculated peak flood, because failures of embankment dams frequently have resulted from inadequate spillway discharge capacity.

In some countries a spillway is designed so that it can discharge the peak floods. As a result, failure of a dam will not occur under the most severe flood conditions that might occur.

Notes

①岩石必须坚固到足以长期暴露在变化的气候和潮湿的环境中不至于断裂。
②修建一座足以预防最罕见的洪水的高坝，通常比修建一条溢洪道要昂贵些。

UNIT ELEVEN

Text   Environmental/Sanitary Engineering

[1]   Environmental/Sanitary engineering is concerned with providing clean, safe water supply systems for towns, cities, and rural areas. It is also concerned with disposing of excess water and waste materials by means of sewer systems. Many aspects of environmental/sanitary engineering are directly related to hydraulic engineering; indeed, some of the projects that we discussed in the previous unit are parts of water supply systems. The Hoover Dam, for example, supplies water to the city of Los Angeles, with which it is connected by a series of canals, tunnels, and aqueducts across the deserts and mountains of the southwestern United States.

[2]   A great deal of archeological evidence has revealed the importance of water supply in the ancient world. Probably the most impressive systems were built by the Romans, whose aqueducts still stand in modern Italy, Spain, France, and Turkey. Rome itself had a water supply estimated at 50 million gallons a day, or about 50 gallons a day for each resident of the city. The water was delivered to fountains, where people collected it in pots and then carried it to their homes; only a few buildings and residences had connections to the main pipelines. Rome also had a sewer, the Cloaca Maxima, part of which is still used today. Like other sewer systems of ancient times, it was intended to carry off the water from storms or the waste water from the public baths. There were penalties for disposing of solid wastes in it.

[3]   After the fall of the Roman Empire, water supply and sewer systems received relatively little attention until modern times. In the Middle Ages in Europe, water came from streams and wells, while wastes were disposed of in cesspools or even returned to the same streams from which the water was taken. After the connection between water supply and certain diseases such as typhoid was established in the nineteenth century, cities and towns all over the world built safe water supply systems. The experience of three American cities illustrates some of the engineering problems—and economic and legal problems as well—in constructing large water supply systems.

[4]   Chicago grew from a tiny trading post on Lake Michigan[①] to a great metropolis in only a few decades. Providing water for the fast growing population was a problem from the city's earliest days. The primary source was the lake that bordered the city, but the water was frequently polluted by discharge of water from Chicago River, which acted as a sort of open sewer during the city's early years. After storms or floods, the pollution was especially severe, and not even moving the pumps for the water farther from the shore[②] was an adequate solution. It was finally decided to reverse the flow of the Chicago River[③] so that it discharged not into the lake but into the Illinois River,[④] a tributary of the Mississippi. After this has been done by means of the Chicago Sanitary and Ship Canal, however, there were cries of outrages, followed by lawsuits, from people in towns and cities downstream from Chicago because their wa-

ter supply sources were being polluted by wastes from Chicago. Finally, the city was forced to build several large sewage treatment plants to remove harmful substances from waste water before it was released into the Chicago River.

[5]　New York City has had to construct a system that brings water to the city from considerable distances. As the city has grown, it has been necessary to range farther and farther away to find new sources. At present, much of New York's water comes from the watershed of the Delaware River, northwest of the city, across the Hudson River and beyond the Catskill Mountains. It is delivered to the city's system of holding reservoirs through the longest tunnel in the world, the Delaware Aqueduct, which extends for the most part through bedrock for a distance of 169 kilometers. At some points the aqueduct reaches a depth of 750 meters. The New York system delivers an average supply of approximately 1.3 billion gallons a day-considerably more than 100 gallons a day for every person in the city.

[6]　Los Angeles is located in an area of low rainfall. When the population of the city began to grow rapidly, water was brought in from the Colorado River, more than 350 kilometers away, across deserts and mountains. The Colorado River Aqueduct, supplying water to Los Angeles and other southern California communities, is 1 081 kilometers long. An even more ambitious project now under construction will divert water from rainy northern California to the drier central and southern portions of the state.

New Words and Expressions

sanitary ['sænitəri]	a.	关于环境卫生的，卫生的
be concerned with		涉及到，与……有关
hydraulic [hai'drɔːlik]	a.	水力的；水力学的；水压的
aqueduct ['ækwidʌkt]	n.	沟渠；导水管；高架渠
reveal [ri'viːl]	v.	泄露；显示
archeological [ɑːkiə'lɔdʒikəl]	a.	考古学的
pipeline ['paip'lain]	n.	管道线；输送管
cloaca [kləu'eikə]	n.	暗渠；下水道；厕所
(pl. cloacae [kləu'eikiː])		
sewer [sjuə]	n.	污水池
cesspool ['sespuːl]	n.	阴沟，污水管，排水管，下水道
metropolis [mi'trɔpəlis]		首都，大城市，文化商业中心
tributary ['tribjutəri]	a.	附属的，（河）支流的
outrage ['autreidʒ]	n.	义愤，痛恨
lawsuit ['lɔːsjuːt]	n.	诉讼
downstream ['daun'striːm]	a.; ad.	顺流的（地）；（在）下游的
sewage ['sju(ː)idʒ]	n.	（阴沟等处的）污水，污物
range [reindʒ]	v.	延伸；探寻；涉及；

watershed ['wɔtəʃed]	n.	流域；集水区
bedrock ['bedrɔk]	n.	基岩
rainfall ['reinfɔ:l]	n.	降雨，降水，降雨量
divert [dai'və:t]	vt.	转移，使转向

Notes

①Lake Michigan [leik'miʃigən] 密执安湖，北美洲五大湖之一。
②全句是一个并列句，…not even moving…from the shore，是后面一句的主语。
③Chicago River 芝加哥河。北美中北部的河流。
④Illinois River [ili'nɔiz] 伊利诺斯河，是美国中北部密西西比河的支流。

Exercises

Reading Comprehension

I. Say whether the following statements are True (T) of False (F) according to the text.

1. Environmental/Sanitary engineering is not concerned with providing clean, safe water supply systems for towns, cities, and rural areas. ( )
2. A large amount of archeological evidence has revealed the importance of water supply systems in the ancient world. ( )
3. After the connection between water supply and certain diseases such as typhoid was established in the nineteenth century, cities and towns all over the world did not build safe water supply systems. ( )
4. The New York system delivers an average supply of approximately 1.3 million gallons a day—considerably more than 100 gallons a day for every person in the city ( )
5. Providing water for the fast growing population was a problem from the city's earliest days. ( )
6. Los Angeles is located in an area of low rainfall. ( )
7. At present much of New York's water comes from the watershed of Chicago River. ( )
8. Finally Chicago was forced to build several large sewage treatment plants to remove harmful substances from waste water before it was released into the Chicago River. ( )
9. The Colorado River Aqueduct, supplying water to Los Angeles and other southern California communities, is 1 081 kilometers long. ( )
10. In the Middle Ages in Europe, water came from streams and rivers, while wastes were disposed of in cesspools or even returned to the same rivers from which the water was

taken. ( )

II. Identify main ideas for each paragraph by matching the following ideas with their appropriate paragraph numbers.

A. In order to meet the people's needs, Chicago had (1)
   to build several large sewage treatment plants.
B. The importance of water supply systems in the (4)
   ancient world.
C. New York City has had to construct a system that (3)
   brings water to the city from considerable distance.
D. Cities and towns all over the world did not build (5)
   safe water supply systems until the nineteenth century.
E. What is environmental/sanitary engineering? (2)

Vocabulary

I. Fill in the blanks with the words or expressions given below. Change the form if necessary.

| construct | reveal | collect | dispose | carry off |
| recycle | connect | extend | supply | divert |

1. Close examination of a lump of soil or the sides of a pit dug through soil profile _____ that soils consist of millions of particles of sand, silt and clay, separated by channels of different sizes.
2. They _____ of the rubbish and make the environment beautiful.
3. Large modern dams are _____ across rivers to store and control vast quantities of water.
4. A ditch _____ water from the stream into the fields.
5. Some kinds of trash can be _____ separately—— glass, newspapers and aluminum cans, for example.
6. The lake _____ the people of the city with a lot of potable water.
7. The soldiers seized the two men and _____ them _____.
8. One modern method of disposing of trash and domestic wastes is _____, which simply means using the waste material again.
9. When the river rises, the water is admitted to these basins through canals that _____ through the river-bank.
10. The Hoover Dam, for example, supplies water to the city of Los Angeles, with which it is _____ by a series of canals, tunnels, and aqueducts across the deserts and mountains of the southwestern United States.

II. Complete each of the following statements with one of the four choices given below.

1. The process of separating solid particles from a fluid with a filter is called _____
   A. permeation   B. circulation   C. filtration   D. continuation
2. The modern trend is to build separate drainage systems for storm runoff and for domestic wastes so that the treatment plants do not have to _____ the runoff water.
   A. flow into   B. carry off   C. dispose of   D. in charge of
3. Some treatment plants fill their own energy needs by burning their waste products to provide steam for _____ .
   A. taking a bath   B. purifying water   C. having warmth   D. generating electricity
4. The water is passed through a filter that consists of a bed of sand or gravel, which _____ a large proportion of the solids that might otherwise contaminate the supply.
   A. participates   B. removes   C. puts   D. goes
5. As New York City has grown, it has been necessary to range farther and farther away to _____ new water sources.
   A. find   B. look   C. take   D. move

Reading Material A

Sanitary Engineering

Part of providing a safe water supply is disposing of the liquid and solid wastes. This problem has become acute in recent years not only because of world-wide population growth, but also because of vast amount of waste created by industrial processes and by the great mountains of trash that are the by-product of increased consumption.

A large number of modern drainage systems use the same sewers to dispose of domestic wastes and runoff water from storms. Many of these systems were designed to empty into streams or other bodies of water where nature itself purified the water over a period of time. Now, however, the amount of waste has become so great that many streams and lakes and even the seas have become polluted. More and more treatment plants are being built to purify water before it is released back into the environment. Therefore, the modern trend is to build separate drainage systems for storm runoff and for domestic wastes so that the treatment plants do not have to process the runoff water, which is relatively unpolluted.

There are a number of different methods by which solid wastes can be removed or rendered harmless. Several of them are ordinarily used in combination in treatment plants. One of the processes is filtration, another is sedimentation, in which wastes are allowed to settle until they become solid or semisolid and can be removed. There are also techniques in which water can be treated by biological means, by using some kinds of bacteria to kill other kinds, or by chemical means, as in chlorination. One of the most successful methods is called the activated sludge process. It involves using compressed air to increase and control the rate of biological reactions that purify the wastes. In effect, treatment plants speed up natural purification processes so that the water that is finally released from them is essentially harmless.① Presentday concern over environmental pollution has increased the demand that waste water should be treated to the fullest degree possible before it is returned to the environment.

Vast amounts of trash have also posed problems in disposal. Much of it has been used as landfill by dumping in swampy areas or in shallow water so that the area can be made useful. A great deal of it has also been burned in incinerators, huge furnaces that reduce the wastes to ash. Incinerators, however, are out of fashion today because they release harmful fumes into the air. Many of them are being redesigned to control these emissions more effectively; at the same time other solutions are being sought.

One modern method of disposing of trash and domestic wastes is recycling, which simply means using the waste material again. The wastes from treatment plants, for example, can be used as fertilizer. It can also be used as fuel. In fact, some treatment plants fill their own energy needs by burning their waste products to provide steam for generating electricity. Similarly, some kinds of trash can be collected separately——glass, newspapers, and aluminum cans, for example. All of these materials can be processed for reuse. In some cases, trash has also been compacted to serve as fuel.

The concern for a cleaner environment together with the need to conserve and reuse our resources has created a challenge for which sanitary engineers, working with environmentalists, will be called upon to find new solutions over the next few years.②

Notes

①实际上，污水处理厂加速了自然净化过程，因此最终从其中排放出去的水基本无害。
②为了一个较清洁的环境以及保护和再利用资源的需要，要求环卫工程师与环保专家一起行动，在今后几年内找到新的解决办法。

Reading Material B

Municipal Engineering

In an industrially underdeveloped country the municipal engineer is sometimes concerned only with simple street maintenance, cleaning and lighting. But in Britain in a town of 100 000 to 500 000 people he might also be in charge of water supply, sewerage and sewage disposal, dwelling and other construction, road building, traffic engineering, public suburban transport, and (before the gas and electricity nationalizations of 1948) also the town gas and electricity supplies.① An exceptional town like Hull has a municipal telephone service. Carlisle has municipal hotels where municipal beer is drunk.

In Britain since about 1950 the supplies of gas and electricity have been provided by nationalized industries which have taken over all the formerly municipal gas or electricity services. In the largest British cities, water supply and public transport to the suburbs have also been taken over by independent corporations. These are not nationalized bodies but are set up for each city by law as the need arises.

Thus the ideal job for an ambitious energetic young municipal engineer is to become the city engineer of a growing town of some 300,000 people where he will be concerned also with the zoning and layouts of factories and municipal housing, and many of the services to them, including the new roads, their gardens or trees, lighting, drainage, water supply, and bus or railway services. The highest social responsibility for this work is in the zoning of the land into areas for heavy industry, light industry, shops and offices, housing, parks and games. This is the work of a town planner, but a planner who originally may have been a civil engineer will practically cease to be one, since planning will have become more important to him.

But before he can become city engineer in a town of over 100,000 people, the ambitious young municipal engineer will at first find work in any municipal engineer's department. He will do whatever work is in progress, make drawings of a street being straightened or an overpass being widened, and will visit it for a few hours when his work allows. In this way, after a few years he will have enough experience to qualify for membership of one of the civil engineering institutions which deal with municipal engineering. In Britain the main ones are the Institutions of Municipal Engineers, of Highway Engineers, of Water Engineers and the Institute of Sewage Purification. But to become a city engineer it is usually essential to be an associate member of the Institution of Civil Engineers, so the ambitious man should join the ICE as well as one or more than one municipal institution. ②

To join these institutions he will have to pass their examinations by studying in his spare time. Then after a few years of study and office work he may be appointed to take charge of some construction work as resident engineer. ③ This will give him valuable experience that he will report in his applications to the institutions and discuss with the examining engineers.

For example if he is working with sewerage section of the Engineer's Department he may have designed and drawn the new layouts for the sewerage of a large area of the town which is being demolished and rebuilt with new and wider streets. He will have drawn the temporary diversion sewers needed to take the sewage flow during the reconstruction, as well as the new permanent sewers and their branches, junctions manholes and any other awkward details. The total of all these drawings will be an appreciable amount of useful work to show to the examiners. If he also works on the site throughout the construction period he will be able to see the mistakes he has made on his drawings, correct those which can be corrected, and remember those which cannot.

In any branch of civil engineering such experience is extremely valuable because it gives an understanding of all sides of the work that is obtained by no one else, and by very few civil engineers.

Notes

①但是在英国，在一个10万到50万人口的城镇里，市政工程师也许要负责给水、污水工程和污水处理，住宅和其他建筑工程，筑路，交通运输工程，郊区公共运输以及（在1948年煤气和电国有化以前）城镇煤气和电的供应。

②但是要成为一个城市工程师，通常需要成为土木工程师学会的一名副会员。所以一个有志向的人除了参加一、两个市政工程学会以外，还应参加土木工程师学会。

③这样经过几年的学习和机关工作，他就可能被任命为驻工地工程师而负责一些施工工作了。

UNIT TWELVE

Text   Ecosystem

[1]   The ecosystem can be a small or large part of the biosphere. It is the joint functioning and dynamic unit of the biotope (inanimate environment) and biocoenosis (plant and animal kingdom) and has a definite material and energy flow.

[2]   Biocoenosis is a group of living organism with a definite spatial distribution which is determined by external environmental factors and the interrelationship among the species. Forests, meadows, moors, marshes, lakes, and seas can all be ecosystems. In different parts of the world, the biosphere consists of natural ecosystems (deciduous forests, savannahs, etc.——depending on climatic factors), semi- cultural (meadows and man-affected forests) and cultural ecosystems (cornland), which are characterized by a definite flora and fauna and constitute a habitat. It is the existence of ecosystems that serves as a basis for life on the earth and the survival of mankind. ①

[3]   The functioning of a terrestrial or aquatic ecosystem is based on the following four components:

1. Abiotic environment (biotope), which is the complex of ecological factors (air, water and soil).

2. Producers (autotrophic components) comprise green plants with chloroplasts (trees, bushes, herbaceous plants, agricultural crops, marine and fresh water algae) that transfer solar energy into chemical energy. They produce organic matter from inorganic matter by accumulating it in the form of carbohydrate, protein and fat. It is only in the presence of an appropriate number of autotrophic organisms, i. e. green plants, that an ecosystem can be regarded as "complete". ② A large area of the earth is at present covered by autotrophic ecosystems. Producers are the starting point in the food chain; the existence of all living things (including man) depends on the existence of producers. The total rate of assimilation of producers is called the gross primary production. Gross primary production involves the total amount of organic matter including the amount of organic matter that the plant consumers in its life processes.

3. Consumers (macro-and microscopic consumers, heterotrophic components) constitute another large group of the following components:

(a) The first group of consumers is formed by green plant-eating (herbivore) animals. They are direct or primary consumers. Primary consumers utilize carbohydrates, proteins and fats accumulated in green plants and by decomposing them, they make the potential energy resource of plants available for animals with other feeding processes.

(b) Indirect consumers or detritus-eaters comprise invertebrate animals in soils and waters.

(c) Carnivore form the "top" of consumers. The existence of consumers is not indispensable for an ecosystem. In an arable land ecosystem (e. g. wheat field) herbivores occur in the form plant of pests. Their activity can be somewhat reduced by integrated protection. In this case the consumer of primary production is man himself.

4. Decay organisms comprise different microscopic organisms, bacteria and fungi. Indirect consumers and microorganisms play a very important role in natural ecosystems. Their task is to return the dead organic matter into the foodcycle. Decomposers are essential components of natural, semi-cultural and cultural ecosystems.

[4] In an ecosystem, self-regulation is very important for maintaining a species, and by adapting itself to the living and inanimate environment the species fluctuates within definite quantitative limits. Ecological buffering systems (self-regulation, inner-regulation) are primarily characteristic of relatively stable ecosystems. Owing to the varied composition of species, the adaptability and relative stability of the entire biocoenosis is greater. Nowadays, self-regulating ecosystems occur only rarely. Even the seemingly undisturbed equilibrium of these is disappearing. Such are the ecosystem of the nature reserves.

[5] In the course of successional development it takes a definite period of time for a certain life community to evolve in a given habitat.③ By passing through numerous stages (each stage corresponds to an individual biocoenosis and biotope, respectively) the whole process of development (series) reaches the so-called terminal community (climax). The terminal community stands in equilibrium with the climatic conditions. It is stable and relatively constant. Under our climatic conditions, the forest is this terminal community.

[6] Ecosystems play an important role in the preservation of species. Several species, especially those with a wide ecological amplitude, occur in more than one ecosystem and within the species, numerous biotopes and different ecotypes evolve. The disappearance of natural and semi- cultural ecosystems endanger the genetic and ecological variability of the species. Collections of varieties in botanic gardens can only partly compensate the losses in genetic variability.

New Words and Expressions

ecosystem [iːkəˈsistəm]	n.	生态系统
biosphere [ˈbaiəsfiə]	n.	生物圈
biotope [ˈbaiətəup]	n.	群落生境
inanimate [inˈænimit]	a.	非动物的
spatial [ˈspeiʃəl]	a.	空间的
biocoenosis [baiəkəuˈenəsis]	n.	生物群落
moor [muə]	n.	荒野；沼
savannah [səˈvænə]	n.	热带大草原
deciduous [diˈsidjuəs]	a.	(在成熟期或一定季节) 脱落的
flora [ˈflɔːrə]	n.	植物群
fauna [ˈfɔːnə]	n.	动物群

habitat ['hæbitæt]	n.	栖息地地
climatic [klai'mætik]	a.	气候的
terrestrial [ti'restriəl]	a.	陆地的
aquatic [ə'kwætik]	a.	水生的
abiotic [ə'baiətik]	a.	非生物的
ecological [i:'kɔlədʒikəl]	a.	生态的
autotrophic [ɔ:tə'trɔfik]	a.	自养的
chloroplast ['klɔrɔplæst]	a.	叶绿体
herbaceous [hə:'beiʃəs]	a.	草本的
carbohydrate ['kɑ:bəu'haidreit]	n.	碳水化合物
assimilation [əsimi'leiʃən]	n.	吸收（作用）
consumer [kən'sjumə]	n.	消费者
heterotrophic [hetərə'trɔfik]	a.	异养的
herbivore [hɑ:'bivərə]	a.	食草的
decompose [di:kəum'pəuz]	vt.	分解
detritus [dɪ'traɪtəs]	n.	腐质
invertebrate [in'və:tibrit]	a.	无脊椎的
carnivore ['kɑ:nivə:]	n.	食肉动物
arable ['ærəbl]	a.	适于耕作的
fluctuate* ['flʌktjueit]	v.	波动，涨落
quantitative ['kwɔntitətiv]	a.	定量的
amplitude ['æmplitju:d]	n.	广大，充足
genetic [dʒi'netik]	a.	遗传的
botanic [bə'tænik]	a.	植物的
compensate ['kɔmpenseit]	vt.	补偿
integrated plant protection		综合植物保护
terminal community		最终群落

Notes

①It is the existence of ecosystems that… the survival of mankind.

"It is … that …" 为强调句型，被强调部分是 the existence of ecosystems。

②It is only in the presence of … can be regarded as "complete"。

本句仍为强调句型，被强调部分是 only in the presence of an appropriate number of autotrophic organisms。

③In the course of successional … evolve in a given habitat。

"it" 在句中是形式主语，真正的主语是后面的动词不定式 for a certain life community to evolve in a given habitats。

Exercises

Reading Comprehension

Ⅰ. Say whether the following statements are True (T) or False (F) according to the text.
1. The ecosystem is the joint functioning and dynamic unit of the inanimate environment and plant and animal kingdom and has a definite material and energy flow. ( )
2. Biocoenosis is a group of living organism with an indefinite spatial distribution which is determined by external environmental factors and the interrelationship among the species. ( )
3. Producers consists of green plants with chloroplasts that transfer solar energy into chemical energy. ( )
4. Decomposers are essential components of natural ecosystems (deciduous forests, savannahs) semi-cultural (meadows and man-affected forests) and cultural ecosystems (cornland). ( )
5. Owing to the varied composition of species, the adaptability and relative stability of the entire biocoenosis is much smaller. ( )
6. The ecosystem can only be a large part of the biosphere. ( )
7. Producers are the starting point in the food chain, the existence of all living things is dependent on the existence of producers. ( )
8. The first group of consumers is formed by herbivore animals. ( )
9. Decay organisms constitute the same microscopic organisms. ( )
10. Collections of varieties in botanic gardens can compensate all the losses in genetic variability. ( )

Ⅱ. Choose the best answer according to the text.
1. It is the existence of ecosystems that serves as a basic _____.
   A. for the survival of all living things including man
   B. for the survival of mankind only
   C. for the survival of life on the earth except man
   D. for the survival of herbivore animals
2. The functioning of a terrestrial or aquatic ecosystem is based on _____.
   A. abiotic environment, producers and consumers
   B. decay organisms, abiotic environment, producers and consumers
   C. abiotic environment, carbohydrate, producers
   D. carbohydrate, protein and fat
3. Indirect consumers or detritus-eaters comprise _____.
   A. green plant-eating animals
   B. carnivores

94

C. microscopic organisms, bacteria and fungi

   D. invertebrate animals in soils and waters

4. In an ecosystem, _____ is very important for maintaining a species.

   A. self-regulation, inner-regulation

   B. inner-regulation

   C. self-regulation

   D. biotope

5. The disappearance of _____ can cause danger to the genetic and ecological variability of the species.

   A. natural ecosystem

   B. semi-cultural and cultural ecosystems

   C. natural and semi-cultural ecosystems

   D. meadows and man-affected forests, cornland

Vocabulary

Ⅰ. Complete the following sentences with some of the words or expressions listed below. Changing the form where necessary.

| bacteria | organism | environment | protein |
| species | existence | occur | genetic |

1. Plankton (浮游生物) is the mass of microscopic _____, both animal and vegetable, which live suspended in water.

2. Microfiltering is able to decrease the quantity of organisms 50 to 90%, depending on the _____.

3. Several species, especially those with a wide ecological amplitude, _____ in more than one ecosystem.

4. The carbon dioxide-oxygen relationship of the algae _____ symbiosis (共生现象) is used in the treatment of waste waters.

5. Different persons have different abilities to adapt to their environment. Adaptability _____ a person's age, activity, state of health and degree of acclimatization to the environmental conditions.

Ⅱ. Complete each of the following statements with one of four choices given below.

1. The heavy metals are toxic to microorganisms because of their ability to tie up the _____ in the key enzyme systems.

   A. carbohydrate   B. bacteria

   C. proteins   D. fat

2. The functioning of a terrestrial or _____ ecosystem is based on four components.

   A. hydraulic   B. aquatic

    C. water   D. plant

3. Green plants with chloroplasts are trees, bushes, herbaceous plants, agricultural crops, marine and _____ algae.
    A. fresh water   B. surface water
    C. ground water   D. waste water

4. Indirect consumers and microorganisms play a very important role in natural _____.
    A. detritus   B. flora
    C. meadow   D. ecosystems

5. Sound-absorbing materials are used to _____ the noise within the room, and vibration-isolation (隔振) materials are used to reduce the transmission of vibration to the walls and floors of the room.
    A. increase   B. add
    C. make   D. reduce

Reading Material A

Problems Due to Plankton-algae

The third group of microscopic aquatic plants are the algae. The algae differ from the fungi and bacteria in their ability to carry out photosynthesis. The algae can utilize the energy in light and do not have to depend upon the oxidation of matter to survive. In fact, the algae evolve oxygen during their growth.

The evolution of oxygen by algae and their production of taste- producing oils have made the algae of extreme interest to the sanitary microbiologists. The oxygen production of algae has been coupled with the oxygen demand of bacteria in the stabilization of sewage in oxidation ponds. On the other hand, the excess growth and death of some algae in water reservoirs has caused the sanitary microbiologist many problems in tastes and odor control.

Definition

There is no clear-cut definition of algae which can satisfy everyone. The simplest definition of algae is that it includes all microscopic plants carrying out true photosynthesis. In this way the photosynthetic bacteria which oxidize hydrogen sulfide are excluded. As will be seen later, this definiti on is naively oversimplified.

Identification

The presence of photosynthetic pigments makes it very easy to identify algae under the microscope.① All identification of algae, and hence classification, is based upon physical characteristics. Unlike fungi, a single observation is normally sufficient for identification.

The Trouble Caused by Algae

In surface waters, in temperate countries, algae, which are almost entirely absent in winter, undergo development, sometimes at an explosive rate, during periods of warm weather.

Many species are able to live in fresh water. They are not generally of significance from the point of view of health, but they can cause trouble in filtration plants by clogging the filters very quickly, unless the latter are supplemented by a flocculation and sedimentation plant upstream.②

Effective micro-straining enables the number of organisms to be reduced by 50 to 90%, depending on the species.

In order to achieve maximum elimination of the microscopic algae by flocculation and sedimentation, it is often necessary, at the same time, to carry out pre-chlorination or a preliminary treatment with chlorine dioxide or ozone.

These algae gather together and form a very dense carpet on the surface of filters (especially slow filters), which obstructs the water from passing through.

The filters may also be clogged by the gases released by phytoplankton, in particular oxygen resulting from photosynthetic reactions; such occurrence can also give rise to difficulties in settling.

Some algae are the cause of unpleasant taste and odours. These may be due to phonolic compounds which react with chlorine to give chlorophenols.

Finally some algae can synthesize toxic metabolites. The toxic metabolites in fresh water do not present any danger to those drinking treated water, since they are not excreted; this means that they are eliminated with the algae during treatment.③ However, they can cause the death of animals drinking the untreated water.

Notes

①光合作用的颜色使我们在显微镜下很容易认出藻类来。
②它们对于人体的健康是无关紧要的。可是它们却会给过滤带来麻烦。除非在其上游增设絮凝及沉淀设备，否则它们会很快堵塞滤池。
③这对于那些饮用处理过的水的人来说并无任何危险，因为在处理过的水中不会有这种毒物分泌出来；也就是说，这些有毒的代谢物随同藻类在水处理过程中被排除了。

Reading Material B

The Death of Microorganisms

The sanitary microbiologist is as interested in the death of microorganisms as he is in their growth. The prime function of the sanitary microbiologist is the prevention of the spread of disease through water, milk, or food on a mass scale. This can be done best by killing the microorganisms before they reach the individual.

Pattern of Death

We have already seen the normal pattern of death in the growth cycle. The pattern of death will follow the sigmoid curve if death is due to a single cause. But if death should be due to several factors, the pattern of death will not follow any special function or mathematical relationship. Normally with multiple death factors the death curve will be a multiple function.

Disinfection

Two of the most misused terms in sanitary microbiology are sterilization and disinfection. Sterilization is the complete destruction of all microbial life, while disinfection is the complete destruction of all pathogenic microorganisms. These two terms are similar but quite different. The most common misuse is by the chemical disinfectant manufacturers who often claim their product sterilizes when it merely disinfects.

Disinfection is usually brought about by chemical agents such as chlorine, phenol, cationic detergents, and the like. These materials can be used to sterilize a biological fluid, but it usually is impractical to do so merely from the material requirements. [1] Disinfection is far more economical and practical.

Disinfection is effective because most of the pathogenic microorganisms are more sensitive microorganisms than the nonpathogens. This is true only in the case of the vegetative cells. The spores and cysts of the pathogens are usually more resistant than vegetative cells of nonpathogens. The rate of killing by a disinfectant is primarily a function of the disinfectant concentration and a characteristic of the microorganism, namely, the point at which the life function is destroyed, as well as temperature. [2] Increasing the disinfectant concentration or the temperature results in increased toxicity by a power function rather than by a simple arithmetic function.

Oxidizing Agents

Chlorine and chlorine derivatives are the most common oxidizing agents used in sanitary engineering. As the concentration of oxidizing agents becomes strong, the proteins undergo denaturation at the amino group. Two other oxidizing agents used in sanitary analyses are permanganate and dichromate. Their toxicity is due primarily to the oxidizing reaction, although chromium is a toxic element in its own right.

Heavy Metals

The heavy metals such as mercury, copper, silver, and arsenic are toxic to microorganisms because of their ability to tie up the proteins in the key enzyme systems. The heavy metallic salts prevent the proteins from reacting normally and even change the charge at certain points from negative to positive, causing repelling reactions rather than attracting reactions.[3] If the concentration of the heavy metal is increased to quite a large amount, the surface of the cell becomes completely coated, preventing materials from entering the cell. Precipitation of the cellular protein may even occur.

pH

One of the best controls on microbial growth is pH. At low pH the hydrogen-ion concentration causes denaturation of the key enzyme proteins. Most microorganisms cannot survive below pH 4.0, but a few sulfate oxidizing bacteria can exist at a pH of 1.0. The same is true of the hydroxyl-ion concentration. As the pH rises over 9.5, the hydroxyl-ion begins to exert a toxic effect. Few, if any, microorganisms can survive above pH 11. Control of pH at either a high or a low range can be used to prevent decomposition of stored waste matter until desired. Actually, pH control is the most significant economic control the sanitary microbiologist has over the growth and death of microorganisms.

Notes

① 这些药剂能够用来给一种生物流体杀菌。不过，仅从实际的需要来看，这种做法通常是行不通的。
② 消毒剂的杀菌速率基本上是消毒的浓度和该微生物的特性（即是其生命功能被破坏的那一点），以及温度三者的函数。
③ 这些重金属盐阻止了蛋白质的正常反应，甚止能把某些点上的负电荷转变为正电荷，从而引起排斥反应而不是吸引反应。

UNIT THIRTEEN

Text Factors Responsible for the Burgeoning Air Pollution Problem

[1]   While, air pollution is not a new phenomenon, it is now apparent that it is one of our most rapidly growing environmental problems. ① What are the factors contributing to this rather recent trend toward deterioration of the air environment? There are three major underlying factors which serve to explain this condition.

[2]   The first factor is population growth. The upward trends in population growth in the United States, since World War II, have indeed been impressive. More people mean more manufactured goods and services. This, in turn, lends to the second factor.

[3]   The second one is expansion in industry and technology. The growth of industrial activity, in the same period, has likewise been remarkable in terms of expansion of existing plant capacity, and the increase in number of new manufacturing establishments. In addition, there has been the introduction of a great number of new processes, methods and products. The nature of the airborne wastes from some of these new technologies was completely unknown until adverse effects on man and his environment suddenly became manifest. New industries and processes introduced on a large scale within recent decades include oxygen lancing in steel production, catalytic cracking of petroleum products, manufacture of copolymers, and nuclear energy. In most cases, the raw materials and by-products waste initially were of unknown toxicity, and knowledge of the methods and procedures for abatement of resulting pollution problems lagged far behind the technology of manufacture. The combination of increasing quantities of atmospheric emissions, including materials of undefined character, compounded the growth and complexity of atmospheric pollution.

[4]   The third one is social changes. Two important social changes occurred during this same period, and served to accelerate the trend of burgeoning air pollution:

1. Urbanization

The unrelenting movement of people from rural sections into urban centers has led to the rapid evolution of cities into large metropolitan complexes. On the East Coast, the expansion of the metropolitan areas of Boston, New York, Philadelphia, Baltimore and Washington, D. C. has resulted in the virtual fusion of the entire region into one large megalopolis. There are no longer the open and sparsely populated spaces between these cities that existed twenty or more years ago. ② Within a few years, over three-fourths of the nation's population will reside in about 1% of the land area. The result of this development is an ever increasing density of population and of industrial and commercial activity. Thus, the producers of airborne pollutants now, more than ever before, reside in close proximity to the potential receptors. Such a juxtaposition greatly increases the frequency and severity of interactions between the two, and makes the goal of acceptable air environment extremely difficult to attain.

2. The other social factor which has indirectly contributed to the intensification of air pollution over relatively recent years has been the rising standard of living which has prevailed during this period. Large segments of the population have been economically able to enjoy a better life, including higher quality of nutrition, housing, transportation, and a variety of labor-saving devices. Few families today are without a car, television set, refrigeration, automatic washing machines and clothes dryer, etc. The vast majority of these conveniences require electric power and this, in part, accounts for the fact that the demand for electric power in the United States doubles every ten years. Most of this power is generated by thermal power plants burning coal or oil. Since the combustion of these fuels produces large volumes of contaminant emissions, the potential for air pollution from this source is rapidly increasing.

[5]   The motor vehicle, on which practically every American family is highly dependent, likewise is another major source of pollutants, which are emitted largely from the internal combustion engine.③

[6]   Modern society produces greater per capita solid refuse than ever before. Greater use of paper, plastic and similar materials for single service containers, and for packaging food and numerous domestic and commercial products of everyday life is placing enormous demands on solid waste disposal facilities. Open burning and incinerators of all types and sizes are emitting air-contaminating combustion products of increasing quantities and chemical complexity.

[7]   Thus, the ability of the general population to afford more comforts, conveniences, and labor-and time-saving machinery, contributes very significantly to air pollution originating from the energy conversion processes which provide the necessary power. Thus, a more affluent and educated society demands a better quality of environment than this country has ever enjoyed, while unsuspectingly contributing indirectly to the very environmental degradation they abhor.

[8]   The combined impact of population growth, expansion in industry and technology and social changes operating in our contemporary society can be regarded as the compounding factors which have resulted in serious degradation of the urban air environment within relatively recent years. In certain metropolitan areas such as New York, Los Angeles, Philadelphia, Chicago and St. Louis, this trend has already reached alarming proportions. In those areas, the rate of pollution very frequently exceeds the capacity of the atmosphere to purify itself by natural processes of dilution and dispersion. During these periods, severe air pollution occurs and is clearly manifested by eye irritation, reduced visibility and other adverse effects.

New Words and Expressions

burgeon ['bə:dʒən]	vt.	发展，展开
deterioration [ditiəriə'reiʃən]	n.	恶化；变质
airborne * ['ɛəbɔ:n]	a.	空中的

adverse effect			反作用；不利影响
manifest ['mænifest]		a.	明显的
		vt.	表明；证明
lance [lɑːns]		v.	用枪刺，刺破
		n.	长矛，喷枪
catalytic [kætə'litik]		a.	催化的
copolymer [kəu'pɔlimə]		n.	共聚物
toxicity [tɔk'sisiti]		n.	毒性，毒力
abatement [ə'beitmənt]		n.	减少；除去
emission [i'miʃən]		n.	散发，发射（物）
unrelenting [ˌʌnri'lentiŋ]		a.	不退让的，不松懈的
fusion * ['fjuʒən]		n.	合并，联合
megalopolis [megə'lɔpəlis]		n.	大城市（由几个城市及郊区连成者）
sparsely ['spɑːsli]		ad.	稀疏地，稀少地
pollutant [pə'luːtənt]		n.	污染物
reside [ri'zaid]		v.	住（留）；属于
in close proximity to			与……靠得很近
juxtaposition [dʒʌkstəpə'siʃən]		n.	并列，并置
severity [si'veriti]		n.	严重性
intensification [intənsifi'keiʃən]		n.	加强，强化
segment ['segmənt]		n.	部分，分布
contaminant [kən'tæminənt]		n.	污染物质，杂质
internal combustion engine			内燃机
per capita			每人口
solid refuse			固体废物，固体垃圾
incinerator [in'sinəreitə]		n.	焚化炉，化灰炉
degradation [degrə'deiʃən]		n.	退化，降低
originate [ə'ridʒineit]		vi.	发起，发生
affluent ['æfluənt]		a.	富足的，丰富
abhor [əb'hɔː]		vt.	憎恨，厌恶
dilution [dai'ljuːʃən]		n.	冲淡，稀释
dispersion [dis'pəːʃən]		n.	分散（作用）弥散
irritation [iri'teiʃən]		n.	刺激，兴奋

Notes

① … it is now apparent that … growing environmental problems.

　it 在句中作形式主语，that 引导主语从句。

② There are no longer the open and … twenty or more years ago.

…that existed twenty or more years ago 为定语从句，修饰 spaces。

③The motor vehicle, on which … the internal combustion engine.

on which practically every American family is highly dependent 为非限制性定语从句，修饰 the motor vehicle。

which are emitted largely from the internal combustion engine。为非限制性定语从句，修饰 pollutants。

Exercises

Reading Comprehension

Ⅰ. Say whether the following statements are True (T) or False (F) according to the text.
1. Though air pollution is not a new phenomenon, it is now clear that it is one of our most rapidly developing environmental problems. ( )
2. The second factor, causing deterioration of the air environment, is population growth. ( )
3. The combination of increasing a large number of atmospheric emissions, compounded the growth and complexity of atmospheric pollution. ( )
4. Two important social changes took place during this same period, and served to speed up the trend of burgeoning air pollution. ( )
5. Still there are the open and sparsely populated spaces between these cities, such as Boston, New York, Philadephia, Baltimore and Washington, D.C. ( )
6. The rising standard of living is the other social factor which has indirectly contributed to the intensification of air pollution relatively recent years. ( )
7. Most of the household appliances, such as washing machines and clothes dryer, require electric power, and this, in part, accounts for the fact that the demand for electric power in the United States doubles every ten years. ( )
8. Modern society produces less per capita solid waste than ever before. ( )
9. A more affluent and educated society demands a better quality of environment, while indirectly leading to the very environmental degradation. ( )
10. In those areas such as New York, Los Angeles, Philadelphia, Chicago, this serious degradation of the urban air environment has already reached alarming proportions. ( )

Ⅱ. Choose the best answer according to the text.
1. The factors contributing to this rather recent trend toward deterioration of the air environment are _____.
   A. population growth, expansion in industry and technology
   B. expansion in industry and technology, social changes
   C. population growth, expansion in industry and technology and social changes

D. population growth, and the growth of industrial activity
2. Within a few years, over _____ of the nation's population will reside in about 1% of the land area.
   A. seventy-five per cent
   B. one third
   C. one-fourth
   D. twenty-five per cent
3. Most of electrical power is produced by thermal power plants _____.
   A. burning wood
   B. burning oil or coal
   C. nuclear power
   D. water power
4. Another major source of pollutants, which are emitted largely from the internal combustion engine is _____.
   A. thermal power plants
   B. water power plants
   C. the motor vehicle
   D. nuclear power plants
5. _____ are the compounding factors which have resulted in serious problem of the urban air pollution.
   A. The combined impact of population growth, expansion in industry and technology and social changes
   B. Greater use of paper, plastic and similar materials
   C. Greater use of comforts, conveniences and labor-and time-saving machinery
   D. Solid waste

Vocabulary

I. Complete the following sentences with some of the or expressions listed below. Changing the form where necessary.

| factor | expansion | accelerate | environment |
| adverse effects | | airborne | exist | electric power |

1. Air pollution has been defined as a condition which is likely to cause _____ in man or his possessions.
2. Weathering of stone in buildings and monuments likewise is _____ by manmade pollution.
3. It may be more appropriate to define air pollutants as those substances which _____ in such concentrations as to cause an unwanted effect.
4. Diesel engines have many uses. They run _____ plants, pump water and other fluids and run air compressors, and so on.
5. If death should be due to several _____, the pattern of death will not follow any special function or mathematical relationship.

II. Complete each of the following statements with one of the four choices given below.
   1. Steam engines are called external-combustion engines—external means "outside", and

_____ means "burning."

   A. fuel
   B. combustion
   C. burn
   D. boiling

2. In the context of _____ control, gaseous pollutants include substances that are gases at normal temperature and pressure as well as vapors of substances that are liquid or solid at normal temperature and pressure.

   A. atmospheric pollution
   B. noise pollution
   C. water pollution
   D. environmental pollution

3. It is called _____ to break up the larger molecules of the heavier liquids in the petroleum mixture into the smaller, lighter molecules of gasoline.

   A. cracks
   B. breaking
   C. apart
   D. cracking

4. In many factories _____ are processed completely automatically by means of computers.

   A. raw matter
   B. crude substance
   C. raw materials
   D. original materials

5. People would never know exactly the nature of the airborne wastes from some of these new technologies before adverse effects on man and his _____ suddenly became manifest.

   A. around
   B. surrounding
   C. world
   D. environment

Reading Material A

The "Killer Smog"

Obviously, air pollution is not a new problem. King Edward II tried to solve the problem of what Eleanor of Aquitaine called "the unendurable smoke" by prohibiting the burning of coal while Parliament was in session. His successors, Richard III and Henry V both took action against smoke, the former by taxation and the latter by forming a commission to study the problem. This was the first of a plethora of commissions, none of which helped reduce the level of air pollution in England. Under Charles II a pamphlet was authored in 1661 by John Evelyn, entitled "Fumifugium or the Inconvenience of Aer and Smoak of London Dissipated, together with some Remedies Humbly Proposed." His suggestions included moving industry to the outskirts of town and establishing green belts around the city. None of his proposals were implemented. A subsequent commission in 1845 suggested, among other solutions to the smoke problems, that locomotives "consume their own smoke." In 1847 this requirement was extended to chimneys and in 1853 it was decreed that offending chimneys be torn down.①

In fact, for all the rhetoric and commissions, there was little action in England, or anywhere else in the industrially developing world, until after World War II. Action was finally prompted in part by two major air pollution episodes where human deaths were directly attributed to high levels of pollutants.

The first of these occurred in Donora, a small steel town (pop. 14,000) in western Pennsylvania. Donora is located in a bend of the Mononganela River and in 1948 had three main industrial plants—a steel mill, a wire mill and a zinc plating plant.

During the last week of October 1948, a heavy smog settled in the area, and a weather inversion prevented the movement of pollutants out of the valley. On Wednesday, the smog became especially intense. It was reported that streamers of carbon appeared to hang motionless in the air and visibility was so poor that ever natives of the area became lost. By Friday, the doctors' offices and hospitals were flooded with calls for medical help. Yet no alarm had been sounded. The Friday Halloween parade was well attended, and a large crowd watched the Saturday afternoon football game between Donora and Monongahela High Schools.

The first death had however occurred at 2 a.m. More followed in quick succession, and by midnight 17 persons were dead. Four more died before the effects of the smog abated. By this time the emergency had been recognized and special medical help was rushed in.

Although the Donora episode helped focus attention on air pollution problems in the United States, it took four more years before England suffered a similar disaster and action was finally taken.[2] The "Killer Smog" of 1952 occurred in London, with meteorological conditions similar to those during the Donora episode. A dense fog at ground level coupled with bitter cold and the smoke from coal burners caused the formation of another infamous "pea souper." This one was more severe than the usual smog however, and lasted for over a week. The smog was so heavy that visibility during daylight hours was cut to only a few meters. Bus conductors had to walk in front of their vehicles to guide them through the streets. Two days after the fog set in, the death rate in London began to soar. Sulfur dioxide concentrations increased to nearly seven times their normal levels and carbon monoxide was twice the normal. It is important, however, to not conclude from the apparent relationship that sulfur dioxides caused the deaths. Many other factors may have been responsible, and the various air pollutants probably acted synergistically to affect the death rate.

Primarily due to these acute episodes in London and Donora, public opinion and concern forced the initial attempts to clean up urban air.

Interestingly, we have difficulty in defining what is clean air. From the scientific standpoint, clean air is composed of the constituents. If we accept this as a definition of clean air, however, we are in trouble, since any naturally occurring suspended material can be called a pollutant, and one never finds such "clean air" in nature. It may thus be more appropriate to define air pollutants as those substances which exist in such concentrations as to cause an unwanted effect. These pollutants can be natural (such as smoke from forest fires) or man-made (such as automobile exhaust) and can be in the form of gases or particulates (liquid or solid particles larger than 1 micrometer).

Notes

① 1853年政府颁布了一条法令：违章的烟囱一律拆除。
② 尽管多诺拉事件在美国引起了公众对空气污染问题的关注，可在四年后英国也遭此劫难之后才采取了一些措施。

Reading Material B

Economic Loss from Air Pollution

Air pollution has been defined as a condition which is likely to cause adverse effects in man or his possessions. The untoward consequences of atmospheric pollution cover a very wide spectrum ranging from material damage to personal discomfort and illness. And many of those may be directly or indirectly measured in terms of monetary loss.

High levels of smoke, soot and other particulates increase the rate of soiling of clothes, house furnishing, displayed merchandise, and interior surfaces such as walls and ceilings. The added expense of frequent cleaning and repainting represents the increased cost of living in a polluted area.

Man is dependent upon plants for his very existence and the man-made atmospheric contaminants adversely affect these vital members of our ecosystem. The nature of injuries to plants by various air pollutants can be conveniently divided into two categories of: (1) visible effects and (2) suppression of growth. They include necrosis, chlorosis, epinasty, silver leaf, and leaf abscission and localized necrosis, etc.① It is recognized that plants are among the most sensitive receptors of air pollution. The type and severity of damage depends on a number of factors including species sensitivity, type of contaminant involved, concentration and time of exposure, and other environmental and horticultural factors. It may be interesting to note that certain types of plants can serve as sensitive indicators of air pollution. The cost of damage to vegetation in the United States has been measured in terms of hundreds of millions of dollars annually, and appears to be rising every year.

Animals who graze in the vicinity of certain pollution sources can suffer severe injury and death. Cattle can ingest sufficient quantities of fluorine from contaminated vegetation surrounding copper smelters or phosphate fertilizer plants to develop fluorosis.②

Sheep grazing in the vicinity of copper smelters have ingested fatal quantities of arsenic. The loss of productivity or death of the livestock is a serious economic loss to the farmer.

Air pollution can also result in deterioration of exposed materials.

The corrosion of certain metals from exposure to combinations of natural and manmade air pollutants, especially SO_2 and acidic gases and mists, can be greatly accelerated. More frequent scaling and painting of bridges and other exposed structures represents an additional cost of living or operating in areas of high air pollution.

Weathering of stone in buildings and monuments likewise is accelerated by manmade pollution. This trend poses a serious threat to the survival of historical monuments and other architectural and art forms exposed to modern urban atmospheres.

The darkening of lead-based white paint by sudden exposure to hydrogen sulfide is a well-known phenomenum. Certain acidic pollutants——gaseous and particulates——such as sulfuric acid or incinerator flyash can severely blister paints or automobiles, opening the way to metal corrosion.③

Ozone can cause accelerated cracking of rubber. Because of the high oxidant content of photochemical air pollution, rubber products such as tires and radiator hoses tend to deteriorate more rapidly in Los Angeles. Oxidants attack the carbon-to-carbon bonds in the rubber which, under tension fails, producing minute cracks.④ Frequent replacement of rubber components and insulators in regions afflicted by photochemical air pollution represents a substantial economic loss.

Fabric likewise can deteriorate from air pollution. For example nylon is subject to attack from sulfur dioxide. Years ago there were several reports of nylon stockings suddenly disappearing from the legs of women living in certain cities! The strength and life of fabrics can be appreciably reduced by certain pollutants. In addition dyes tend to fade more quickly in regions of high air pollution.

In general it can be said that real estate property in areas with excessive atmospheric pollution becomes devaluated more rapidly than normal. The sum total of the adverse effects on individuals and property in high pollution zones makes these areas less desirable and therefore relatively less valuable. It has been reported that the total estimable economic loss from air pollution in the United States is about $12 billion dollars per year.

Notes

①包括黑斑病，褪绿病，偏上性，银叶病，叶脱落和局部组织细胞坏死等。
②牛会由于从炼铜厂或磷肥厂周围被污染的植物中摄取大量的氟而发生氟中毒。
③某些气体或微粒酸性污染物，如硫酸或焚化炉飞灰，能严重地使油漆或汽车起泡，为金属腐蚀大开方便之门。
④氧化剂破坏了橡胶制品中碳-碳键，使橡胶制品绷紧时破裂产生细裂纹。

UNIT FOURTEEN

Text   Solid Waste Disposal

[1]   Solid and hazardous waste may be treated or processed prior to final disposal. Waste treatment or processing offers several advantages. First, it can serve to reduce the total volume and weight of material that requires disposal. It can also change the form of the waste and improve it hanging characteristics. ① Garbage and other organic wastes, for example, can be rendered inoffensive and even useful by a process called composting. Finally, processing can serve to recover natural resources and energy in the waste material, for recycling or reuse. Much of the "waste" material can actually be used as raw material for productive purposes. However, a basic disadvantage inherent in any waste processing or recovery system is the additional cost of constructing and operating the facility.

[2]   One of the most effective methods to reduce the volume and weight of solid waste is to burn it in a properly designed furnace, under suitable temperature and operating conditions. This process is called incineration. It is expensive, and unless appropriate air cleaning devices are provided, atmospheric pollution from the discharge of gaseous and particulate combustion products can occur. It also is a process that requires high-level technical supervision and skilled employees for proper operation and maintenance.

[3]   The advantages of incineration, however, often overweight these disadvantages. Incineration can reduce the total volume of ordinary refuse by more than 80 percent. In densely populated urban areas, where large sites suitable for landfilling are not available within reasonable hauling distances, incineration may be the only economical option for solid waste . management. ② In some cases it is feasible to design and operate the incinerator so that heat from combustion can be recovered and used to produce steam or electricity. Incineration may also be used to destroy certain types of hazardous waste material.

[4]   Heat recovery and reuse from MSW (municipal solid waste) incineration is an attractive waste management option from an environmental and ecological perspective. But the problems just mentioned, along with the very high costs for equipment and controls, the need for skilled technical personnel, and the need for auxiliary fuel system, can make it a less attractive option.

[5]   Incineration without heat recovery is simpler to manage and can be less than one third as costly as recovery system. Nevertheless, plain incineration does result in a total loss of recoverable energy. Because of public and political interest in "recycling", there will probably be an increasing emphasis on the design and construction of MSW heat recovery systems in the coming years. Incineration, with or without heat recovery, is becoming more "attractive" for solid waste management than burial of MSW in a landfill since suitable sites for burial of solid waste are becoming increasingly difficult to find.

[6]　Another relatively new development in MSW treatment by thermal-chemical conversion is a process known as pyrolysis, which is also called destructive distillation. It differs from conventional incineration in that it is an endothermic process, that is, it requires continuous input of heat energy to occur.③ (Incineration, on the other hand, is an exothermic process which gives off heat as oxidation occurs).

[7]　Pyrolysis is a high-temperature process (1 100 ℃ or 2 000°F) which takes place in a low-oxygen or oxygen-free environment. Combustion of natural gas is used to start the process, but if about 70 percent of the gaseous pyrolysis by-products are recycled back to the gas burners, the process can become self-sustaining.

[8]　Instead of combustion, pyrolysis involves a complex series of chemical reactions. These reaction decompose or convert the organic carbon components of the solid waste into potentially useful by-products. Pyrolysis also substantially reduces the volume of the solid waste. The gaseous, liquid, and solid by-products of pyrolysis include methane, methanol, tar and charcoal. They are combustible and can be used as fuels, or they can serve as raw materials for other synthetic chemical products.

[9]　The actual composition of pyrolysis end-products may vary, and it is very dependent on the nature of the solid waste as well as on the temperature and pressure under which the process operates. The quality of the by-products can be significantly improved if glass, metal, and other inorganic material is first removed or separated from the solid waste that is fed into the pyrolysis furnace. Although waste separation adds to the expense, the pyrolysis process still has great potential as an effective solid waste management method. In addition to reducing waste volume and producing useful by-products, it poses less of a threat to air quality than does incineration.④

New Words and Expressions

hazardous * ['hæzədəs]	a.	有害的
handling characteristics		处理特性
garbage ['gɑːbidʒ]	n.	垃圾；废料
serve to		用于……
inoffensive [ˌinə'fensiv]	a.	无害的
inherent * [ˌin'hiərənt]	a.	固有的；内在的
compost [kɔm'pɔst]	vt.	把……做成堆肥
raw material		原材料
incineration [inˌsinə'reiʃən]	n.	焚化
particulate combustion products		颗粒燃烧物
supervision [sjuːpə'viʒən]	n.	监督；管理
overweight ['əuvə'weit]	vt.	在重量上超过
densely [densli]	ad.	密集地；稠密地

landfill [lændfil]	vi.	土地掩埋
haul [hɔ:l]	vt.	用力拖（或拉）
option ['ɔpʃən]	n.	选择；选择权
municipal solid waste (MSW)		城市固体废物
ecological perspective		生态学观点
recoverable [ri'kʌvərəbl]	a.	可重获的；可找到的
burial [beriəl]	n.	埋葬
pyrolysis [pai'rɔlisis]	n.	热解作用
pyrolysis furnace		干馏炉；热解炉
distructive * [dis'trʌktiv]	a.	破坏性的
destructive distillation		分解蒸馏；干馏
endothermic [endou'θə:mik]	a.	吸热的
exothermic [eksəu'θə:mik]	a.	放热的
oxygen-free environment		无氧环境
self-sustaining [selfsəs'teiniŋ]	a.	自给的
methane ['mi:θein]	n.	（化）甲烷
methanol ['meθənɔl]	n.	（化）甲醇
tar [tɑ:]	n.	焦油
combustible * [kəm'bʌstəbl]	a.	可燃的；易燃的
pose * [pəuz]	vt.	造成；形成

Notes

①It can also change the form of the waste and improve it handing characteristics.

主语 It 表示 waste treatment；句中第二个 it 指代 "the waste"，废物。"它（废物处理）也可改变废物的形式和改造废物的处理特性。"

②…, where large sites suitable for landfilling…

where 引导的非限制性定语从句修饰 areas。

③It differs from…in which it is an endothermic process, …

in which 是关系代词加介词引导一个定语从句修饰 incineration。当指物时，介词后的关系代词只能用 which，that is 是插入语，it requires continuous… 是修饰 endothermic process 的非限制性定语从句。

④In addition to reducing…than does incineration.

by-products 意为 "副产品"；poses a threat to 意为 "对……造成威胁"；

句中 it 指代前一句中 pyrolysis "热解作用"。

…than does incineration 是倒装句，does 指代 poses 以避免重复。

Exercises

Reading Comprehension

I. Say whether each of the following statements are true (T) or false (F) according to the text.
1. Before final disposal, solid and hazardous waste may be treated or processed. ( )
2. Waste treatment or processing offers only one advantage. ( )
3. By a process called composting, garbage and other organic wastes can be rendered offensive and even useless. ( )
4. The process of incineration is to reduce the volume and weight of solid waste which is burnt in a properly designed furnace. ( )
5. The process of incineration requires neither high-level technical supervision nor skilled employees for proper operation and maintenance. ( )
6. The disadvantages of incineration, however, often overweight the advantages of that. ( )
7. Incineration can reduce the total volume of ordinary refuse by less than 80 percent. ( )
8. Incineration without heat recovery is simpler to manage and can be more than one third as costly as recovery system. ( )
9. The quality of the by-products can be improved by first removling glass, metal and other inorganic material in the pyrolysis furnace. ( )
10. Although waste separation adds to the expense, the pyrolysis process still has great potential as an effective solid waste management method. ( )

II. Choose the best answer according to the text.
1. _____ can serve to reduce the total volume and weight of material that requires disposal.
   A. Raw material treatment or processing
   B. Solid waste treatment or processing
   C. Sewage Purification
   D. Air purification
2. Natural resources and energy _____ can be recovered by waste treatment or processing.
   A. in the air   B. in the sea
   C. in the waste material   D. in the sky
3. Under _____ temperature and operating conditions, the volume and weight of solid waste can be reduced.
   A. high   B. low   C. cold   D. proper

4. _____ pyrolysis poses less of a threat to air quality than does incineration.
   A. Except reducing waste volume and producing useful by-products
   B. Besides reducing waste volume and producing useless by-products
   C. Except increasing waste volume and producing useful by-products
   D. Besides reducing waste volume and producing useful by-products
5. Pyrosis involves a complex series of chemical reactions _____ combustion.
   A. in addition to   B. instead of
   C. in spite of   D. in place

Vocabulary

I. Complete the following sentences with some of the words listed below, changing the form where necessary.

oxidation;	hazardous;	combustible;	raw material;	potential;
methane;	option			

1. It is reported that there are lots of _____ particulates in the air.
2. There is a great _____ in pyrolysis process, though it adds to the expense.
3. Incineration may be the only economical _____ for solid waste management in densely populated urban areas.
4. By-products of pyrolysis from gaseous, liquid and solid are _____ and can be used as fuels.
5. An exothermic process which gives off heat as _____ occurs is called incineration.

II. Complete each of the following statements with one of the four choices given below.
1. The consequence resulting from the air pollution _____ show the importance of taking preventive measures.
   A. solved to   B. served to   C. posed to   D. compost to
2. More emphasis must also be given to reuse and recovery of waste so that these materials can be _____ as raw materials.
   A. reacted   B. recorded   C. recited   D. recycled
3. Pyrolysis is a high-temperature process which _____ in a low-oxygen or oxygen-free environment.
   A. takes place   B. takes the place
   C. takes place of   D. takes a place
4. _____ it is feasible to keep the air from being polluted by purifying it.
   A. In some case   B. In case of
   C. In some cases   D. In cases of
5. The temperature today will _____ from 15℃ to 25℃.
   A. very   B. vary   C. verify   D. verge

Reading Material A

Where Do Pollutions Come from?

(1) Sewage and Industrial Wastes

As a result of pollution, Lake Erie, on the borders of the U.S.A. and Canada, is now without any form of aquatic life.

Pollution in water is not simply a matter of highly concentrated "poisons" killing large numbers of fish overnight. ① Very often the effects of pollution are not noticed for many months or years because the first organisms to be affected are either plants or plankton. But these organisms are the food of fish and birds and other aquatic creatures. When this food disappears, the fish and birds die too. In this way a whole food chain can be wiped out, and it is not until dead fish and water birds are seen at the river's edge or on the sea shore that people realize what is happening. ②

Where do the pollutants come from? There are two main sources—sewage and industrial waste. As more detergent is used in the home, so more of it is finally discharged with the sewage into our rivers, lakes and seas. Detergents harm water birds by dissolving the natural fatty substances which keep their feathers waterproof. ③ Sewage itself, if it is not properly treated, contaminates the water and prevents all forms of life in rivers and the sea from receiving the oxygen they need. Industrial waste is even more harmful since it contains compounds of copper, lead, zinc and nickel, all of which are highly toxic to many forms of aquatic life. ④

So, if we want to stop this pollution, the answer is simple: sewage and industrial waste must be purified. It may already be too late to save some rivers and lakes, but others can still be saved if the correct action is taken at once.

(2) Radio-active Pollution

Every country needs more electrical power; coal is getting uneconomical to use, oil is expensive, and we can't rely on natural gas forever. So atomic power stations will be the thing of the future. But there are some sorts of dangers directly connected with nuclear power station, such as radiation and atomic waste. At Windscale, there was an accidental escape of radiation which affected a large area around the power station a few years ago. All the milk produced on farms in the area had to be thrown away because it wasn't safe to drink. Atomic waste is either dumped at sea or buried underground. But there's no way of really knowing when the containers which hold it will disintegrate. ⑤ Some radio-active substances have a half-life of thousands of years, and the containers may only last one or two hundred years.

Nuclear power stations are, at the moment, a very small, almost insignificant source of the radio-activity found all over the world. Our world is more radio-active than it should be because we have exploded too many nuclear bombs in it. As we learn more and more about radiation and the illnesses it can cause (which are often undetectable until twenty or thirty years after exposure), we find that we are constantly having to lower the so-called "safe dose" of radiation that anyone can be exposed to.⑥

Strontium 90, which is only produced by artificial nuclear fission, is so widespread that most countries regularly check how much there is in milk supplies. The cows producing the milk take in Strontium 90 from the grass they eat.

But it isn't only land animals that are affected by Strontium 90. When some marine algae were tested at Plymouth, on the south-west coast of England, they were found to contain between twenty and forty times more Strontium 90 than the sea water around them.⑦ Such radio-activity can be passed along food chains, getting more and more concentrated, until the fish or sea birds die, or are eaten by man.⑧

Notes

① 对水质的污染不只是一件高度浓缩的毒物一夜间杀死大量鱼类的事情。
highly-concentrated "poisons" killing large numbers of fish overnight 是带有逻辑主语的动名词结构，作介词 of 的宾语。

② ……人们直到在河边和海岸上看见死鱼和死水鸟时才意识到正在发生什么事情。
what is happening 是宾语从句。

③ 去污剂通过溶解水鸟身上能保持羽毛防水特性的天然脂肪质来伤害水鸟。
1) dissolving the natural fatty substances which keep their feathers waterproof 是动名词短语，作介词 by 的宾语。
2) which keep their feathers waterproof 是定语从句，修饰 substances。

④ 工业废物甚至更为有害，因为它含有铜、铅、锌和镍等化合物，而所有这些化合物对许多水生生物都有剧毒。
all of which are highly toxic to many forms of aquatic life 是由代词（或名词）+of+which 引出的非限制性定语从句，修饰 compounds。

⑤ 但是没有任何方法真正知道装原子废渣的容器什么时候破裂。
1) really knowing when the containers which hold it will disintegrate 是动名词短语，作介词 of 的宾语。
2) when the containers which hold it will disintegrate 是宾语从句，作动名词 knowing 的宾语。
3) which hold it 是宾语从句，修饰 containers。

⑥ 由于我们越来越多地了解有关辐射以及由它所引起的疾病的知识（那些疾病在二、三十年内常常不易被人发现），我们现在不得不经常降低一个人所允许接受的所谓辐射"安全剂量"。

⑦ 在普里茅斯城，对某些海藻进行了测试，发现这些海藻所含的锶 90 为其周围海水所含锶 90 的 20 至 40 倍。

⑧那样的放射性能通过食物链传递，聚积得越来越浓缩，直到鱼类和海鸟死掉，或者被人类吃掉。

"getting more and more concentrated" 为现在分词短语作状语，表示伴随状况。

Reading Material B

Industry Sludges

Paper Industry Sludges

All industrial sludges should not be judged as hazardous materials having a serious impact on the environment. ① Industrial sludges generated by Michigan's paper industries currently are being handled by several deferent methods. The paper industry is a good example of diversity in sludge disposal methods. Several different approaches have been implemented with a minimum of difficulty and, in most cases, no adverse environmental problems.

Paper industry plants are scattered throughout the state of Michigan with no specific sector considered a predominant location. ② Disposal of sludges by the paper industry varies for each plant, with a host of factors considered significant in establishing a preferred method. ③ As one might expect, there are many factors and considerations that determine the final method of disposal. In the case of the paper industry, a significant consideration must be given to economics. Since the paper industry is extremely competitive, economics must be weighed carefully in considering disposal of sludges.

The weather is a definite consideration in selecting a disposal method. A good number of paper mills utilize land application of sludges. This is an excellent method except during inclement weather conditions in the spring and fall when sludge cannot be placed on the land, prompting the need for good storage facilities. Some disadvantages arise withthe use of storage facilities, such as the potential for odor nuisances and the need to handle the sludge more than once.

Although land disposal is a favored method, an Alpena Paper Mill is building a large dryer facility to remove moisture from the sludge to enable its utilization as a fuel source in plant operations. With rising fuel costs, it is conceivable that more consideration will be given to this method of disposal in future. Some disadvantages to this approach are environmental concerns, the high capital expenditure, operational expenses and fuel cost for the drying process. These disadvantages need to be balanced with the favorable features of low handling costs, low transportation costs and the lack of land disposal areas.

Metal Industry Sludges

Metal sludges used to be discarded in the most convenient location available to the industry. The various methods included disposal into lagoons on plant premises, in landfills, into public owned treatment works and by incineration. By today's standards, each of these practices is excluded from consideration because of its adverse environmental side effects.

Chemical Industry

Sludges from the chemical industry represent a high level of concern because of their extreme toxicity and ability to cause or contribute to acute or chronic adverse effects on human health. Currently, these solids are being disposed of in many ways, there is some amount of recovery, some are being treated chemically for neutralization, some are solidified for landfills, and some of the more toxic sludges are being incinerated.

While incineration is preferable for the very toxic organic chemicals, Michigan is very deficient in high-temperature incinerators that are equipped with pollution control systems and have adequate retention times. There are few incinerators available in the state to handle contaminated sludges. As a rule, companies with facilities now in operation will not accept contaminated sludges for commercial disposal.

Where companies have attempted to use existing incinerator facilities to rid society of some contaminated sludges, citizens objections have overridden such action. A case in point is a cement plant in the Detroit area that sought a permit to burn polychlorinated biphenyl (PCB) in its kiln as part of a routine cement production operation. After public hearings and a two-year effort to obtain a permit, the company finally abandoned any hope of obtaining it, this is most unfortunate because state officials believed that no better method could be obtained to handle the thousands of pounds of contaminated materials now in storage.

One chemical firm in the state had an extraordinary perception of the eventual difficulty in the disposal of toxic and hazardous materials and built a high-temperature rotary kiln. This Misland-based company is one of a very few companies that has the ability to rid itself of hazardous sludges from its manufacturing processes. Its incinerator has been in operation for approximately seven years.

Notes

①不应该把所有的工业废渣都看成是对环境有严重影响的有害物质。
　　having a serious impact on the environment 为分词短语，作定语修饰 hazardous materials。
②…with no specific sector considered a predominant location。
③…, with a host of factors considered significant in establishing a preferred method。

这两个结构是分词独立结构前面加上介词 with，构成"with＋名词词组＋-ed 分词"，即带有复杂宾语的介词词组。这种结构有时也由"with＋名词词组＋ad."或"with＋名词词组＋a."等构成。这种结构通常表示伴随状况或补充说明，有时也有时间，条件，原因等意义。例如：

1) With the tree grown tall, we get more shade.
2) They sat in the room with the curtains drawn.
3) he slept in the classroom with the light on.
4) They were having a meeting in the room with the window closed (open).

UNIT FIFTEEN

Text   Combating Water Pollution

[1]   Effective pollution control systems depend on policies that combine technical, economic, social, and aesthetic considerations. The decisions involved require answers to many complex questions. How can we provide water of what quality, when, how much, to what people, and for what purposes?① Who is to be restrained from putting how much of what kinds of wastes into what parts of the water system? Who is to be permitted to use waters for waste disposal and under what terms and conditions? Who will pay the high cost of protecting surface and groundwaters?

[2]   The extreme view of demanding absolutely clean or pure water is as unacceptable as uncontrolled water pollution, since technical and financial feasibility must be included in all practical considerations of the problem.

[3]   There are several ways in which water pollution can be combated. First, through treatment of wastewater to make water reusable and of high quality.② Second, by the enactment and enforcement of governmental regulations prohibiting and limiting pollution of waters. Third, by development of practices and techniques that will prevent or limit the natural runoff of pollutants—for example, from agricultural areas—into water.

[4]   The traditional method of controlling water pollution in the United States has been to collect waste in a system of sewers and transport it to a waste treatment plant where the wastewater is treated for discharge into streams and for reuse.

[5]   There are two kinds of sewer systems—combined and separate. Combined sewers carry both water polluted by human use and storm water polluted as it drains off homes, streets, or land. In separate systems, sanitary sewers carry only sewage, while storm sewers carry the large volumes of storm runoff water. During dry weather when combined sewers are handling only the normal amount of wastewater, all of it is carried to the waste treatment plant. But, during a storm, when combined sewers have to carry a much larger amount of water, part of the water, including varying amounts of raw sewage, often bypass the treatment plant and flow directly into receiving streams. In theses cases, the process of dilution is depended on to minimize the pollution, but this is a highly undesirable situation.

[6]   Wastewater is usually treated by two processes, called primary and secondary treatments. In primary treatment, solids are allowed to settle out from the water, and the effluent from the tank is then treated by chlorination to kill disease-causing bacteria and reduce odors. Although 30% of the municipalities in the United States give sewage only primary treatment, this process is inadequate for most water needs. In secondary treatment, up to 90% of organic material in sewage is removed simply by making use of the bacteria in the organic material. In this process the effluent leaving sedimentation tanks is acted on by bacteria that consume a sub-

stantial amount of the organic material in the sewage. Secondary treatment is completed by the addition of chlorine, which kills more than 90% of harmful bacteria in the effluent. In a very few areas, notably near Lake Tahoe, water is subjected to advanced tertiary treatment involving many new processes that further purify the water.③

[7] In areas lacking a sewer system or treatment plant, lagoons or septic tanks are used. A septic tank receives wastewater from home and holds it while bacteria in the sewage break down the organic material so that clearer water flows out into a leaching field. Lagoons that provide for proper depth and detention while sunlight, algae and oxygen interact can also restore water to a quality equal to that provided by the standard secondary treatment.

New Words and Expressions

aesthetic [iːsˈθetik]	a.	美学的
restrain ... from (doing)		制止……（干）……
waste disposal		废物处理
feasibility * [fiːzəˈbiliti]	n.	可行性
enactment [inˈæktmənt]	n.	颁布
enforcement [inˈfɔːsmənt]	n.	实施
combined sewer (system)		合流制下水管（系统）
separated sewer (system)		分流制下水管（系统）
drain off		把……排除
bypass [ˈbai-pɑːs]	vt.	越过，绕……走
minimize [ˈminimaiz]	vt.	使减少到最少
dilute [daiˈljuːt]	vt.	冲淡
settle out		沉淀出来
municipality [mju(ː)nisiˈpæliti]	n.	市；市政府
undesirable * [ˌʌndiˈzaiərəbl]	a.	讨厌的；令人不快的
inadequate [inˈædikwit]	a.	不足的；不适当的
be acted on		受……作用
notably [ˈnəutəbli]	ad.	显著地；著名地
tertiary [ˈtəːʃəri]	a.	第三级的
leach [liːtʃ]	vt.	滤去（物质）
leaching field		渗滤场
septic [ˈseptik]	a.	引起腐烂的
septic tank		化粪池
detention [diˈtenʃən]	n.	滞留
interact [ˌintərˈækt]	vi.	互相作用；互相影响

Notes

①How can we provide…and for what purposes?

此句是用逗号将五个分句连接起来的并列句。其中后四个分句为省略句，省略了与前一分句相同的主语 we 及谓语 can provide。

②First, through treatment of wastewater…and of high quality.

这是一个省略句，相当于 First, water pollution can be combated through treatment…以下 second 及 third 仿此。

③…involving many new processes that…

此介词短语为状语，其"involving"相当于"including"。

Exercises

Reading Comprehension

I. Say whether each of the following statements are True (T) or False (F) according to the text.

1. The extreme view of demanding absolutely clean or pure water is as acceptable as uncontrolled water pollution. ( )
2. There is only one way in which water pollution can be combated. ( )
3. Combined sewers carry not only water polluted by human use but also storm water polluted as it drains off homes, streets, or land. ( )
4. In separate systems, storm sewers carry only sewage, while sanitary sewers carry the large volumes of storm runoff water. ( )
5. During a storm when the combined sewers are carrying only the normal amount of wastewater, all of it is carried to the waste treatment plant. ( )
6. In the wastewater treatment, there are two processes called primary and secondary treatments. ( )
7. In secondary treatment, less than 90% of organic material in sewage is removed simply by making use of the bacteria in the organic material. ( )
8. In a very few areas, water is subjected to advanced tertiary treatment, including many new processes that further purify the water. ( )
9. In some areas lacking sewers systems or treatment plants, septic tanks or lagoons are usually used. ( )
10. A septic tank receives wastewater from home and keeps it while bacteria in the sewage break down the organic material so that clearer water flows out into another septic tank. ( )

II. Choose the best answer according to the text.

1. Effective pollution control systems depend on _____ that combine technical, economic, social, and aesthetic considerations.
   A. methods　　　　B. problems　　　　C. policics　　　　D. experiences.
2. In practical consideration of the water pollution, we must _____.
   A. demand absolutely clean or pure water
   B. take both technical and financial feasibility into account
   C. control the use of water by human beings
   D. prevent the polluted water from spreading
3. In primary treatment, in order to _____ in water, we may use chlorination.
   A. develop disease-causing bacteria and reduce odors
   B. get rid of disease-causing bacteria and reduce odors
   C. develop disease-causing bacteria and remain odors
   D. find out disease-causing bacteria and odors
4. Preventing and limiting pollution of waters by the enactment and enforcement of governmental regulations is _____ to combat water pollution.
   A. the best way　　　　　　B. the only way
   C. the worst way　　　　　 D. one of the ways
5. Although 30% of the municipalities in the United States give sewage only primary treatment, this process is _____.
   A. inadequate for most water needs
   B. adequate for most water needs
   C. inadequate for least water needs
   D. adequate for least water needs

Vocabulary

I. Complete the following sentences with some of the words or expressions listed below, changing the form where necessary.

| detention;　　pollutant;　　feasibility;　　enactment;　　waste disposal;　　effluent |
| dilution;　　sedimentation; |

1. Scientists are trying to get valuable information as to the _____ of the human being living on the Moon.
2. They are very seriously concerned about the problem of _____ involved.
3. The natural runoff of _____ must be controlled sooner or later.
4. In order to help protect and enhance the quality of water, there are various technical procedures other than wastewater treatment, such as _____.
5. Lagoons that provide for proper depth and _____ can also restore water to a quality

equal to that provided by the standard secondary treatment.

II. Complete each of the following statements with one of the four choices given below.
1. There are several factors which can _____ us _____ combating water pollution.
   A. restrain ··· with ···   B. restrain ··· from ···
   C. restrain ··· to ···   D. restrain ··· on ···
2. As a test the metal was _____ great heat.
   A. subject into   B. subjected to
   C. subjecting to   D. subjected into
3. More emphasis must also be given to _____ and recovery of waste so that these material can be recycled as raw materials.
   A. refusal   B. resume   C. reverse   D. reuse
4. The standard thermal units, the calorie and the British thermal unit (BTU) are _____ water.
   A. based by   B. based with   C. based on   D. based at
5. In primary treatment, solids are allowed to _____ from the water.
   A. work out   B. pick out   C. choose out   D. settle out

Reading Material A

Ozone

Ozone is a minor constituent of the atmosphere. it occurs mainly in the stratosphere, at altitudes from 15 to 50 km above the earth's surface and plays a key role, for the well-being of mankind, in filtering out much of the ultraviolet radiation approaching earth from space.① The concentration of ozone in the stratosphere is subject to considerable variation with latitude, longitude and altitude, but basically is governed by a dynamic equilibrium involving oxygen and a number of other gases present in trace quantities. Among the most significant of this group are chlorofluoro hydrocarbons, which are used as aerosol spray propellants, refrigerants and foaming agents for plastics. When released, these compounds will lead to the formation of chemical species which catalyze the destruction of ozone. The chief implications of a reduction in stratospheric ozone is that more ultraviolet radiation would reach Earth, perhaps affecting climates and significantly increasing rates of skin cancer. Since the danger was recognized, action has been taken in the United States and in the European Economic Community to effect a decrease in the use of chlorofluorocarbons as aerosol propellants.② However there has been a small but significant increase in other applications and, more worryingly, production rates in other areas of the world have increased noticeably. Clearly, in a global problem of this kind, effective action must be taken worldwide.③ Also monitoring and research programmes must include any materials which may affect the ozone concentration in a similar manner, for instance other halogenated organic compounds, methane and nitrogen oxides. ④

The difficulty in setting proper air quality criteria for ozone is that ozone is a natural trace gas of the troposphere with average concentrations of 20-40 ppb All the assessment studies indicate that health effects and, in particular, damage to the vegetation occur close to levels of the natural background concentration of ozone.

The toxicological experiments indicate that higher than ambient doses of ozone may have an impact on the biochemical activity of the blood, reduce pulmonary function, and increase general respiratory discomfort. Ozone damages the membranes surrounding pulmonary capillaries and causes pulmonary edema. Compared to human beings, trees and plants are obviously even more susceptible to ozone concentrations higher than the natural background concentration. The effects of ozone in plants are often proportional to dosage (concentration × exposure time), i. e. there is a no-threshold dose response. ⑤ Concentration of twice the natural background concentration of ozone can produce reductions in growth or yield.

Besides its damaging effect on humans and vegetation, ozone may also cause damage to fibers, dyes, paints and other organic materials. In fact, natural rubber and synthetic polymers suffer from a deterioration of the mechanical structure by the action of ozone. Ozone reacts with double bonds in organic material. In this process, the material cracks and becomes brittle. Regarding the degradation of rubber and other elastomers by ozone, the prevention or retardation of this process by means of antiozonant additives is of great interest. Photochemical oxidants also damage exterior household paints and pigments and consequently, are a major hazard to works of art.

National ambient air quality standards for photochemical oxidants were first established in the U. S. in 1971. This value, measured as ozone, was initially set at an hourly average concentration not to exceed 80 ppb more than once per year. ⑥ At that time, ozone concentration in rural and remote area were believed to be low relative to the standard. Furthermore, the U. S. Environmental Protection Agency (EPA) decided to refer the health and welfare standard for photochemical air pollution exclusively on ozone, rather than on total oxidants. Since air quality standards generally contain a built-in safety factor, which is on the order of 3-5 for health effects, the value of 80 ppb was in line with common practice. However, subsequent studies of the ozone concentration in rural areas as well as on transport phenomena throughout world have shown that ozone is almost unique as an air pollutant, because the line between harmless and harmful is very narrow, probably more so for ozone than for any other air pollutant. In response to these finding, the EPA promulgated in 1979 a revised ambient air quality standard for ozone stating that the expected number of days per calendar year with daily maximum ozone concentrations exceeding 120 p. p. b. must be one. ⑦ Some air quality goals and standards for ozone have now been established in several countries.

Notes

①at altitudes from … 是介词短语作定语。修饰 stratosphere；in filtering…是介词短语作状语。全句意为：它主要存在于地球表面上的海拔高度 15 至 50 公里处的平气流层中，对人类的健康起着重要的作用，它能过滤掉从太空到达地球上的大部分的紫外线。

②动词不定式短语 to effect…在句中作目的状语，主句为被动形式，这是当主语不明确时，常采用的形式。全句意为：美国及欧洲共同体已采取了行动，以减少作为火箭推进剂的氯氟烃的使用。

③Clearly, in a global … be taken worldwide.
句中 in 意为"对于"，表示动作对象。全句意为：显然，对于这种全球性的问题，必须在全世界范围内采取有效的措施。

④监测和研究方案也必须包括那些可能以类似方法影响臭氧浓度的物质，如其他的卤化有机物、甲烷和氮的氧化物。
这里 in similar manner 是指与氯氟烃影响臭氧浓度的方式相似。

⑤臭氧对植物的影响常与剂量（浓度×曝露时间）成比例，也就是说没有一个临界剂量响应值。

⑥more than once 不止一次；hourly average concentration 小时平均浓度。
全句意为：作为臭氧的测量值最初被定为：小时平均浓度不超过 80 ppb 的次数每年不止一次。

⑦针对这些发现，环境保护局于 1979 年颁布了经过修改的臭氧环境空气质量标准，该标准要求每历年日最大臭氧浓度超过 120 ppb 天数只能是一天。

Reading Material B

Acid Rain

All over Europe, and in North American, there are lakes and forests which are dead or dying and the cause is thought to be acid rain.① Furthermore, it may become much more widely spread—for acid rain is likely to occur wherever fossil fuels are intensively used. What is acid rain? Mr. Justin Cook, a scientist explains: All fossil fuels, that is oil, coal and gas, contain sulfur. When these are burnt, for example, in motor vehicles, they form sulfuric acid. This goes up into the air, and soon it falls back to earth, into lakes and onto trees in forests. As a result, lakes become acidic, fish disappear and trees are killed. The pollution is carried great distances by the wind, so sulfuric acid produced in Britain and travel as far as Scandinavia.

Lakes and rivers were the first victims of acid rain. As the water becomes more acid, the amount of aluminum in it starts to increase rapidly. Concentrations as low as 0.2 milligrams per liter of the metal in acid water kill fish. Large scale fish kills have been recorded in some

Swedish lakes, and these have been attributed to aluminum poisoning rather than to high acidity alone. ②

Soils are normally much better able to resist acidification than lakes, rivers and streams, and so can take much more acid without noticeable ecological drawbacks. Their vulnerability differs depending on their type, the kind of bedrock they cover, and the use to which man puts them. The most vulnerable lands are those that have bedrocks poor in lime, covered with shallow layers of soil containing low concentrations of protective substances. Large parts of Scandinavia are like this.

As well as the health of important ecosystem, human health may also be put at risk by pollution. ③ High concentrations of sulphur dioxide, nitrogen, oxides and dust have long been known to be harmful. This issue is only marginally related to the problem of acid rain, since such concentrations are usually only found close to the sources of pollution, and sulphur oxide levels in many European and North American cities have been decreasing recently.

Other, indirect, health hazards are suspected. These would be caused by the metals like lead, copper, zinc, cadmium and mercury released from soils and sediments by increased acidification. They can get into groundwater, rivers, lakes and streams used for drinking water, and be taken up in food chains leading ultimately to man. The releases of cadmium in particular may give rise to a growing problem as acidity increases, as normal levels in human food are already close to the acceptable daily intake. It seems that the risks arises as soon as the acidity of the water rises above normal. ④

Meanwhile, acid accelerates corrosion in most materials used in the construction of buildings, bridges, dams, industrial equipment, water supply networks, underground storage tanks, hydroelectric turbines, and power and telecommunications cables. In can also severely damage ancient monuments, historic buildings, sculptures, ornaments and other important cultural objects. Some of the world's greatest cultural treasures, including the Parthenon in Athens and Trojan's column in Rome, are being eaten away by acid fallout. ⑤

Coal contains two kinds of sulphur-pyrite (iron sulphide) and organic sulphur. Washing coal, after first crushing and grinding it, will remove pyrite sulphur. The cost of this mechanical process is estimated to be $1 to $6 per ton of coal. On average it will remove about half of the pyrite, though "at best" the process can be made to remove up to 90 per cent of it from some coals. the chemical methods are more effective, but also more expensive and have not yet been fully developed. They can remove organic sulfur as well as pyrite.

Notes

①定语从句 which are dead or dying 中，dead 是形容词，意为"已经死的"；而 dying 是 die 的现在分词，所以 which are dying 是一般现在时，表示"正在死亡；濒临死亡"。

②kill 在此是名词，rather than 用于进行选择，这一表达方式常用在"平行结构"里，即与两个名词、代词或形容词等连用。全句意为：据记载瑞典的某些湖里已有大量的鱼死亡，

这不仅只是由于酸度高而主要是因为铝中毒。
③As well as…是比较状语，在此意为："与……一样"，全句意为：与重要的生态系统的健康一样，人类的健康也在污染的威胁之下。
④It seems that，意为"看起来似乎"，that the risks arises 是主语从句，全句意为：当水的酸度超过正常标准，看来就会产生危险。
⑤主句中的谓语是 are being eaten away by acid fall-out，是现在进行时的被动态，全句意为：世界上一些最珍贵的文化瑰宝，包括雅典的帕提农神庙和罗马的图拉真圆柱，都正受到酸沉降物的侵蚀。

UNIT SIXTEEN

Text   Paving the Way to Excellence in Water Supply System

[1] Excellence is a goal meant to be persistently quested rather than completely achieved. ①

[2] The supply to human communities of something as vital and precious as water has always been the enterprise whose main objectives are guided by the satisfaction of a need. The way society sees this need commands the way responsible suppliers and authorities embrace the indispensable tasks of their jobs. ②

[3] Historically, the achievement of this goal has gone through three stages, correspondent to certain degrees of socio-economical and cultural development: (i) the quantity stage, where the bare satisfaction of biophysical needs is the main task; (ii) the quality stage, in which psychological, cultural, and aesthetic goals join the biophysical ones; (iii) the excellence stage, meant to add to the quality stage the touch of sustainable social, economical, and environmental features.

[4] In this evolution, human beings begin to be considered as mere arithmetical figures (percentage of population supplied), turn into consumers during the quality stage, to finish as real managing partners in the excellence stage.

[5] The world of water supply provides us with examples of all the above stages. Where conditions of poor coverage of population have to be faced as top priority in many parts of the world, quality of service does not come first and has to give place to quantitative and hygienic problems. ③

[6] On the other hand, there is a clear indication everywhere of the increasing importance of problems characteristic of the upper boundary between the two latter stages.

[7] Customer awareness is nowadays an indisputable factor on developing both business strategies and field operational programmers. For example, South African suppliers re thinking very much in customer terms today, and we learned only last May that Japanese attitudes have changed because of the Kobe earthquake and the criticism that resulted from the lack of customer information.

[8] In Portugal, a significant positive evolution has been observed over the last 20 years, with 77% of the population currently connected to public systems, and a target of 95% by the year 2000.

[9] An official nationwide survey published three years ago, based on simplified criteria, indicates that 40% of the population supplied are thought to enjoy a good service, 54% an adequate service, and 6% a poor service.

[10] The quality of the service provided to the consumers becomes from now on a funda-

mental issue, particularly with regard to continuity of supply, water quality and reliability.

[11]   Working for excellence is therefore a challenge and a must for the Portuguese water industry.

[12]   Significant capital investments are expected to be carried out during the forthcoming years in order to improve the current levels of service, with the emphasis on a correct establishment of priorities and development of a new culture towards management efficiency and consumer satisfaction. A wide variety of measures of national scope is clearly required, including the definition of a coherent framework for sustainable development in the forthcoming decades.

[13]   A number of initiatives aiming at contributing to the goal can currently be recognized, such a the publication of new legislation, the implementation of National and European funding schemes, and development of applied research focusing on the tools to support the technical management of water utilities.

[14]   The assessment of levels-of-service on a national basis is far from being a widespread practice. England and Wales are perhaps the best existing examples, and much can be learnt from their experience; nevertheless, there are major underlying distinctions between this case and the situation in other countries, such as Portugal, where the water utilities tend to be managed by local authorities, and the institutional framework is organized differently. In general, water undertakers are of a small size and have a lower technical and financial capacity. The total privatization of water supply and wastewater utilities introduces another key element that cannot be underestimated.

[15]   A wide set of new concepts had to be developed aiming at the use of levels-of-service as management tools rather than simple, coarse inspection or control instructions for financial purposes only.

[16]   The perspective under which the framework illustrated in this paper has been focused may be characterized as an integrated, sustainable element of management-supportive strategy. The main body targeted remains the operating entity, no matter the nature of the company: public, private or combined.

New Words and Expressions

persistently [pə(:)ˈsistəntli]	ad.	不断地；坚持地
quest [kwest]	vi.	追求；探索
enterprise * [ˈentəpraiz]	n.	（艰巨，复杂或冒险性的）事业；企业单位
correspondent [ˌkɔrisˈpɔndənt]	a.	符合的；一致的
biophysical [ˈbaiəuˈfizikəl]	a.	生物物理学的
arithmetical [ˌæriθˈmetikəl]	a.	算术的
coverage * [ˈkʌvəridʒ]	n.	覆盖率
priority * [praiˈɔriti]	n.	重点；优先

quantitative *	[ˈkwɔntitətiv]	a.	数量的；定量的
hygienic	[haiˈdʒi:nik]	a.	卫生的；卫生学的
awareness *	[əˈwɛənis]	n.	觉醒；意识
indisputable	[ˈindisˈpju:təbl]	a.	无可争辩的；无可置疑的
programmer *	[ˈprəugræmə]	n.	规划；订计划者
Kobe	[ˈkəubi]	n.	神户（日本港市）
Portugal	[ˈpɔ:tjugəl]	n.	葡萄牙（欧洲）
nationwide	[ˈneiʃənˈwaid]	a.	全国性的
criterion	[kraiˈtiəriən]	n.	（批评，判断的）标准；准则
（复）criteria	[kraiˈtiəriə]		
continuity *	[ˌkɔntiˈnju(:)iti]	n.	连续（性）；持续（性）
forthcoming	[fɔ:θˈkʌmiŋ]	a.	即将到来的；即将出现的
coherent *	[kəuˈhiərənt]	a.	一致的；粘附的
sustainable	[səsˈteinəbl]	a.	持续的；能忍受的
initiative	[iˈniʃiətiv]	n.	倡议；首创精神
legislation	[ˌledʒisˈleiʃən]	n.	立法；法规
implementation *	[ˌimplimenˈteiʃən]	n.	履行；实施
assessment	[əˈsesmənt]	n.	评估；估价
Wales	[weilz]	n.	威尔士（英国）
underlying *	[ˌʌndəˈlaiiŋ]	a.	根本的；基础的
institutional	[ˌinstiˈtju:ʃənəl]	a.	制度上的；惯例的
undertaker	[ˌʌndəˈteikə]	n.	承担者；承办人
water undertaker			自来水厂
privatization	[ˌpraivitiˈzeiʃən]	n.	私有化
inspection	[inˈspekʃən]	n.	检查；视察
characterize *	[ˈkæriktəraiz]	vt.	表示……特性；描写……的特性
integrate *	[ˈintigreit]	vt.	使……成一整体
entity	[ˈentiti]	n.	实体；统一体

Notes

①… meant to be persistently quested rather than completely achieved.
   为过去分词短语作定语修饰"goal"；rather than 为并列连词，连接 quested 和 achieved 两个分词。

②The way … commands the way …
   the way 可当从属连词用，引导一个省略关系副词 that 或介词加关系代词 inwhich 的方式分词；the way-方式分句相当于 how-和 as-方式分句。注意：用了 the way 就不能再接 how-或 as-分句。如：

That's　　　　how she spoke.
　　　　　　the way (that) she spoke.
　　　　　　*the way how she spoke.
The steak is cooked just how/as/the way I like it.

③Where conditions of poor coverage of … quality of service … hygienic problems. where 为关系副词引导状语从句。

④characteristic of 为形容词短语，修饰 problems，意为：属于后两个阶段之间的较高要求的问题…

Exercises

Reading Comprehension

I. Say whether each of the following statement sare True (T) or False (F) according to the text.

1. Excellence is a goal which people seek continuously and can be completely achieved. 　　　　　　　　　　　　　　　　　　　　　　　　　　　　　　( )
2. To supply vital and precious water to human communities has always been the enterprise whose main purposes lie in the satisfaction of a need. ( )
3. In addition to the biophysical one, psychological, cultural, and aesthetic goals are included in the quantity stage. ( )
4. Human beings turn into real managing partners in the excellence stage. ( )
5. Quality of service should come first where there is a poor coverage of population. 　　　　　　　　　　　　　　　　　　　　　　　　　　　　　　( )
6. An official nationwide survey published three years ago, indicates that vast population supplied are thought to enjoy a good service. ( )
7. Significant capital investments are expected to be carried out during the forthcoming years in order to improve the water supply system. ( )
8. In order to improve the current levels of service, a wide variety of "measures" of national scope is clearly required. ( )
9. In Portugal, the water utilities tend to be managed by local authorities, and the institutional framework is organized the same as England and Wales. ( )
10. In order to use levels-of-service as management tools rather than simple, coarse inspection or control instructions for financial purposes only, a wide set of new concepts had to be developed. ( )

II. Choose the best answer according to the text.

1. In _____, psychological, cultural and aesthetic goals join the biophysical ones.
   A. the quantity stage　　　　　　　　B. the excellence stage
   C. the quality stage　　　　　　　　　D. the supply stage

2. In the evolution, human beings turn into _____ during the quality stage.
   A. partners   B. consumers   C. managers   D. controllers
3. Japanese attitudes have changed because of the Kobe earthquake and criticism that resulted from _____.
   A. lack of water-supply information   B. lack of customer information
   C. lack of earthquake information   D. lack of management information
4. In Portugal, _____ of the population currently have connected to public systems and a target of _____ by the year 200.
   A. 70%…90%   B. 80%…95%
   C. 77%…100%   D. 77%…95%
5. From now on, in Portugal, _____ becomes a fundamental issue.
   A. the water supply systems   B. the quality of the service
   C. the hygienic problems   D. the quantitative problems

Vocabulary

I. Complete the following sentences with some of the words or expressions listed below, changing the form where necessary.

correspondent to,	command,	rather than,
connect … to …,	with regard to,	characteristic of,
provide … with …,	integrate…with	

1. It ought to be quantity and hygiene _____ quality of service that come first where there are conditions of poor coverage of population.
2. Water supply should _____ quality of service _____ quantity of service.
3. The development of water supply should _____ certain degrees of socio-economical and cultural development.
4. There is a clear indication of increasing problems _____ traffic accidents in the city.
5. If you want to get more information from the world, you may _____ your computer _____ the international network.

II. Complete each of the following statements with one of the four choices given below.
1. It's reported that 90% of the population in the area _____ good service of water supply.
   A. entitle   B. enable   C. enjoy   D. entreat
2. Great change have been _____ over the last 10 years.
   A. watched   B. looked   C. noticed   D. observed
3. The quality of the service _____ the consumers becomes from now on a fundamental issue.
   A. provided to   B. provided with   C. provides to   D. provides with

4. Excellence in water supply systems is _____ a goal meant to be persistently quested rather than completely achieved.
   A. characterized by   B. characterized as
   C. characterized to   D. characterized in
5. Customer's requirements are nowadays a noticeable factor _____ developing the water-supply.
   A. at   B. in   C. on   D. to

Reading Material A

Control of Data Quality

One of the key aspects of a national framework for assessing levels of service is the quality control of the information produced and reported. This is a particularly difficult matter when the starting point is a generalised lack of good planning and operational data in most water utilities.

The data quality may be controlled in different ways, the main alternatives being (i) Centralised collection, processing, archiving and reporting by a national regulating body, which controls the information reported internally; (ii) Data collection, processing, archiving and reporting by an external and accredited body, which controls the information reported; (iii) Self-control by the water undertakers, in the scope of certified processes; (iv) Self-control by the undertakers in the scope of uncertified processes, audited by independent and authorised bodies.

Alternatives (iii) and (iv) are the most attractive. Self-control is an essential step towards the creation of a culture of excellence within the water utilities. Furthermore, these alternatives do not require the creation of heavy centralised structures, which always tend to become highly bureaucratic and inefficient.

Process certification is ideally the best solution. However, it is not realistic to expect every process required for assessment of levels-of-service to be certified by every water company within an acceptable time. Consequently, the procedure recommended is as follows:

* Water utilities should be responsible for obtaining the data required and for controlling their quality
* Process certification should be encouraged whenever technically and economically feasible;
* For all the other cases, external audits are strongly recommended.

Whenever the municipalities decide to contract the management of water supply systems to external entities, the appointment of independent auditors should be a licence condition.

Definition of guidelines for auditor qualification is therefore a very important issue to be developed during the implementation phase.

Confidence grading scheme

A confidence grading scheme will have to be developed in order to allow the users of the levels-of-service reports to know how much they can trust the information available. This aspect was carefully developed in England and Wales, and there is no evidence at this stage that it is not adequate for the Portuguese case.

Confidence grades

The confidence trades will need to provide a reasoned basis for the operating entities to double check information with the auditor (s), as regards reliability and accuracy.[1]

It is essential that proper care and a high level of application is given by the operating entity and their auditor to the assignment of confidence grades to data.

A quality-assured approach should be employed in the methodology used to assign confidence grades, particularly if sampling techniques are in place. Confidence grades should reflect the current status of the data, not the future status that it is intended to achieve.

Reliability bands

A. Highly Reliable. Actual-Data based on sound records, procedures, investigations or analyses which are properly documented and recognised as the best methods of assessment. Forecasts—Based on extrapolations of high quality records covering or applicable to 100% of the operating entity's area, kept and updated for a minimum of five years (the forecast will have been reviewed during the reporting period.)[2]

B. Reliable. Actual-Generally as "A", but with minor shortcomings, e. g.: some of the documentation is missing, the assessment is old, or some reliance on unconfirmed reports or some extrapolation are made. Forecasts -Based on extrapolations of records covering of applicable to more than 50% of the operating entity's area, kept and updated for a minimum of five years. The forecast will have been reviewed during the past two years.

C. Unreliable. Actual-Data based on extrapolation from a limited sample for which Grade A or B is available. Forecasts-Based on extrapolations of records covering more than 30% of the operating entity's area. The forecast will have been reviewed during the previous five years.

D. Highly Unreliable. Actual-Data based on unconfirmed verbal reports and or cursory inspections of analysis. Forecasts-Based on extrapolated information not complying with bands A, B, or C.

Notes

①信任等级需要为经营实体提供就可靠性和准确性与审计者重复核对资料的理性基础。
②以百分之百覆盖或适用于经营实体地区的高质量记录的推断为基础的预告,且至少保持五年并更新(在报告期该预告应予复查)。

Reading Material B

The Monitoring Approach of the Levels-of-service Framework

The monitoring philosophy underlying the levels-of-service framework presented in this paper is believed to be acceptable by many water service undertakers in the working in a region where socio-economical development, sector guidelines, and customer habits are similar in Portugal.

This approach is not intended to be a mere academic exercise, but a useful tool leading water suppliers to decision pathways representing the customer's expectations.

The central idea of an enlarged vision of the customer as a human being playing an important role within a very wide spectrum opens a vast field of new social, economic, and environmental needs and problems seldom included in actual current management plans and action programs.

The ideas contained in the methodology described here will take some time to enter the boardroom of the Portuguese water utilities and a little longer to seep through their whole operating services.

The reaction of the public is perhaps going to be swifter than expected, due to the growing awareness of consumers to the quality of the water services provided to them, and may act as a warning light to incredulous or slow-reacting managers.

The authors believe that the new ideas contained in the evaluation exercise (e.g. the extension of the concept of "consumer") together with the presence of some modern trends applied to water utilities performance impact (e.g. effects on ecological and cultural environments), will bring some successful practical examples in the near future.

Since an aspect of this methodology is to produce useful management and public awareness information from the indicators data, it is important to make some provisions for data quality control and data reporting procedures. In this particular aspect, the major contribution of the work developed is thought to be the definition of criteria for aggregating the high number of existing water utilities for reporting purposes, so as to balance the need for an easily real message and the potential use of the information.①

· The role of all the actors involved in the water market, apart from the consumer and the regulating and operating bodies, will be of noticeable importance in the implementation and improvement of this type of assessment scheme: private operators, national or international nongovernmental organizations, as well as experts, consultants, manufacturers, etc., must be integrated in the whole process.②

Notes

①人们认为，目前在这方面所开展的工作其主要贡献是为因报告目的而大量收集现有给水设施资料确定了标准，以此达到对简而易读的信息的需要与对资料的潜在利用之间的平衡。

②在实施和改进这种评估计划中除消费者和经营管理机构外，所有供水市场涉及者的作用将会明显的重要：私人经营者、国家或国际非政府组织、以及专家、顾问、制造商等等，他们必须在整个过程中结合为一个整体。

Appendix I Vocabulary

abatement *n.* 减少,除去	13
abhor *v.* 憎恨,厌恶	13
abiotic *a.* 非生物的	12
acceleration *n.* 加速(度,作用)	10
acetic *a.* 醋(乙)酸的	08
aceti cacid 醋(乙)酸	08
acidity *n.* 酸性(度)	05
activated carbon 活性炭	05
adjacent * *a.* 邻近的,相邻的	09
address oneself to… 论述,谈判	08
adverse effect 反作用	13
aeration *n.* 曝气,通气	09
aesthetic *a.* 审美的,美学的	15
affluent *a.* 富足的,丰富的	13
air conditioning equipment 空调设备	06
airborne * *a.* 空中的	13
alarming *a.* 令人注目的	03
alchemist *n.* 炼金术士	01
alkaline *n.*; *a.* 碱性;碱性的	05
alkalinity *n.* (强)碱性	05
algae *n.* (*pl. alga*) 藻类,海藻	02
amplitude *n.* 广大,充足	12
anaerobic *a.* 厌氧的,厌气的	08
appurtenance *n.* (常用 *pl.*) 附属物,设备;配件;附属建筑(装置)	07
aquatic *a.* 水的,水性的	12
aqueduct *n.* 沟渠;导水管;高架渠	01
aquifer *n.* 蓄(含)水层	09
arable *a.* 适于耕作的	12
archeological *a.* 考古学的	11
arithmetical *a.* 算术的	16
ascertain * *v.* 确定,查明	05
as it does 实际上	08
assessment *n.* 估价,评估	16
assimilation *n.* 吸收(作用)	12
assume *v.* 呈现(某种形式)	03
atmospheric *a.* 大气(中)的,空气的	08
attack *v.* (化学)腐蚀,锈蚀	08
autotrophic *a.* 自养的	12
awareness * *n.* 觉醒,意识	16
bacteriological *a.* 细菌学的	05
bacteriology *n.* 细菌学	03
Bangladesh *n.* 孟加拉国	03
barrage *n.* 拦河坝	04
basin *n.* 水池,水槽	01
be acted on 受…作用	15
be brought up to 使(或被)……达到	04
bedrock *n.* 基石	11
be exposed to 成为……受害者	03
before proceeding 首先	10
be multiplied by 乘以	06
biochemical *a.* 生物化学的	08
biocoenosis *n.* 生物群落	12
biophysical *a.* 生物物理学的	16
biosphere *n.* 生物圈	12
biotope *n.* 群落生境	12
botanic *a.* 植物的	12
brackish *a.* 稍咸的,(水)含盐的	04
breakdown *n.* 分解,分离	08
break-point chlorination 折点加氯	05
burgeon *v.* 发展,展开	13
burial *n.* 埋葬	14
butyric *a.* 丁酸的,奶油的(丁酸)	08
butyricacid 丁酸	08
bypass * *v.* 越过,侥……走,回避	15
calculation *n.* 计算,统计	08

词条	释义	章节
capillary n.; a.	毛细管（的）	09
carbohydrate n.	碳水化合物	12
carnivore n.	食肉动物	12
catalytic a.	催化的	13
catch basin	收集池，沉水池	01
catchment n.	集水（量），汇水	06
catchment area	集水区	06
cellulose n.	纤维素	05
cesspool n.	污水池	11
chaos n.	混乱，泛滥	03
characterize * v.	表示……特性；描写……的特性	16
chlorinate v.	（使）氯化，用氯消毒	04
chlorine * n.	氯（气）	05
chlorine dioxide	二氧化氯	05
chlorophenols n.	氯酚	05
chloroplast n.	叶绿体	12
cholera n.	霍乱	03
circulatory a.	循环的，流通的	07
cistern n.	蓄水池，贮水器	01
clarification n.	澄清，净化	01
climatic a.	气候的	12
cloaca n. (pl. cloacae)	暗渠；下水道；厕所	11
coagulant n.	凝结剂，凝结剂	01
coagulation n.	凝聚作用，凝结物	01
coalesce v.	凝聚	05
coefficient * n.	系数	09
coherent * a.	一致的；粘附的	16
colloidal a.	胶体（状，质）的	05
combat v.	和…作斗争，反对	05
combined sewer	合流制，下水管（系统）	15
combustible * a.	可燃的，易燃的	14
come from	由于	06
compaction n.	压实，压缩	09
compensate v.	补尝	12
component n.	分（力，量，支）	10
the component of the gravity force	重力的分量	10
compost v.	把……做成堆肥，施堆肥于	14
compressor * n.	压缩机	06
concerned a.	有关的	06
be concerned with	与……有关的	11
conducive a.	有助于……的，促进的	04
be conducive to	对……有益的	04
conductivity * n.	传导性	05
conduit n.	导管，水管（渠）	10
confines n. (pl.)	界线,范围,边界	10
congregate v.	聚集	02
constancy n.	（不变,恒定,持久)性	10
constituent n.	组成物，构成物	04
consumer * n.	消费者；用户	12
contaminant * n.	污染物质，杂质	02
contaminate v.	污染，弄脏	02
continuity * n.	连续(性)；持续(性)	16
copolymer n.	共聚物	13
correspondent a.	符合的；一致的	16
corrosive a.	腐蚀的	05
coverage * n.	覆盖率	16
criterion (pl. criteria) n.	（批评,判断的)标准;准则	16
cross-connection n.	交叉连接	07
culture n.	培养，养殖	08
culture media	培养基	08
curve n.	曲线	10
backwater curve	回水曲线，壅水曲线	10
deciduous a.	（在成熟或一定季节）脱落的	12
decolorize v.	漂白	05
decompose * v.	分解；使腐烂	12
degradation n.	退化，降低	13
densely ad.	密集地，稠密地	14
derivative a.	转生的,派生的,衍生的	08
designate v.	表示，称为	02
destructive distillation	分解蒸馏，干馏	14
detention n.	停滞，滞留	15
deteriorate v.	变质，损坏	07

deterioration	n. 恶化，变质	13
detract *	v. 降低，减损	05
detritus	n. 腐质	12
dilute	v. 冲淡，稀释	15
dilution	n. 冲淡，稀释	13
discharge	n. 排泄（水气），排出物	03
dispersion *	n. 分散（作用），弥散	13
distillation	n. 蒸馏法	01
distill	v. 蒸馏	04
distribution reservoir	配水库（池）	06
distribution system	配水系统	06
distribution pipe	配水管道	06
divert	v. 转移，使转向	11
downstream	a.; ad. 顺流的（地）；在下游的	11
drain off	把……排除	15
drainage	n. 排水；排水设备；排出的水	01
earthen	a. 土制的	01
ecological	a. 生态的	12
ecological perspective	生态学观点	14
ecosystem	n. 生态系统	12
ecotype	n. 生态型	12
effluent	a. 流出的；n. 流出物，污水，废水	03
electrodialysis	n. 电渗析	04
elevation	n. 高度，海拔	10
emission	n. 散发，发射（物）	13
enactment	n. 颁布，法令	15
endothermic	a. 吸热的	14
enforcement	n. 实施，执行	15
enterprise *	n. （艰巨，复杂或冒险性的）事业	16
entity	n. 实体；统一体	16
epidemic	n. 流行病，时疫	03
estuary	n. 河水，海湾	04
esturaine	a. 河口的，港湾的	04
Ethiopia	n. 埃塞俄比亚	03
evaporation	n. 蒸发	06
evaporation water	蒸发水	06
exemplify	v. 举例说明，作为……的例子	08
exothermic	a. 放热的	14
fall a prey to (＝suffer from)	成为……牺牲品	02
fauna	n. 动物群	12
feasibility *	n. 可能性，可行性	12
fermentation	n. 发酵	08
filtration *	n. 过滤	01
floc	n. 絮体，絮凝物体	04
flocculate	v. 絮凝，绒聚	04
flocculating agent	絮凝剂	04
flora	n. 植物群	12
fluctuate *	v. 波动，涨落	12
formation	n. 地（岩）层	06
forthcoming	a. 即将到来的；即将出现的	16
foul *	a. 污浊的	01
fringe	n. 边缘，端	09
fungi	n. 真菌	05
fusion *	n. 合并，联合	13
garbage	n. 垃圾，废料	14
genetic	a. 遗传的	12
germinate	v. 使发芽，萌芽	03
gradient *	n. 梯度，斜度	09
grate	v. 装格栅于	01
guideline	n. 准则	03
habitat	n. 栖息地；产地	12
handling characteristic	处理特性	14
haul	v. 用力拖（或拉）	14
hazardous *	a. 有害的，危险的	14
herbaceous	a. 草本的	12
herbivore	a. 食草的	12
heterotrophic	a. 异养的	12
high demands	高峰用水量	06
hundreds of times as large as	比……大几百倍	06
hydraulic *	a. 水力的；水力学的；水压的	01

英文	词性	中文	页
hydrological	a.	水文学的	02
hygienic	a.	卫生的；卫生学的	16
implementation *	n.	履行；实施	16
impounding	v.	贮（水）备灌溉用	06
impounding reservoir		蓄水池	06
inadequate	a.	不充足的；不适当的	15
inanimate	a.	非动物的	12
incinerator	n.	焚化炉，化灰炉	13
in close proximity to		与……靠得很近	13
independently of		与……无关,不去决于	08
indisputable	a.	无可争辩的，无可置疑的	16
infiltration	n.	渗透（入）	06
infiltration water		渗透水	06
inherent *	a.	固有的，内在的	14
initiative	n.	倡议，首创精神	16
injurious	a.	有害的	04
inlet	n.	进（气，水）口	07
inoffensive	a.	无害的	14
inorganics	n.	无机物	02
inscription	n.	（铭）刻，碑文	01
inspection	n.	检查，视察	16
institutional	a.	制度上的，惯例的	16
integrate *	v.	使成整体，使一体化	16
integrated plant protection		综合植物保护	12
in tensification	n.	加强，强化	13
interact	v.	互相作用，互相影响	15
intergranular	a.	（颗）粒间的	09
intermolecular	a.	分子间的	09
internal combustion engine		内燃机	13
intruth		实际上，说实在话	08
invertebrate	a.	无脊椎的	12
iron	n.	离子	09
irrigation	n.	灌溉（注）	10
irritation	n.	刺激，兴奋	09
juxtaposition	n.	并列，并置	13
Kobe	n.	神户	16
lagoon, lagune	n.	污泥（水）池，氧化塘	01
lactic (lactic acid)	a.	乳的（乳酸）	08
laminar	a.	层（式，状，流）的	10
lance	v.	用枪刺，刺破	
	n.	长矛，喷枪	13
landfill	v.; n.	土地掩埋	14
lawsuit	n.	诉讼	11
lay down		制定，提出	03
leach	v.	滤去（物质）	15
leaching field		渗滤场	15
legislation	n.	立法，法规	16
limestone	n.	石灰石	06
limestone formation		石灰岩层	06
lore	n.	（专门的）知识，（特殊的）学问	01
make sure that		确保	06
malodorous	a.	恶臭的	05
manifest	a.;v.	明显的；表明，证明	13
marsh	n.	沼泽；湿地	12
mastic	n.	胶粘剂	05
medium	n.	介质，培养基	02
megalopolis	n.	大城市	13
methane	n.	甲烷；沼气	14
methanol	n.	甲醇	14
metropolis	n.	大城市,文化商业中心	11
metropolitan	a.	大城市的	02
microbial	a.	微生物的，细菌的	02
microorganism	n.	微生物	02
microbe	n.	微生物，细菌	08
minimize *	v.	使减到最少，使缩到最小	15
modification	n.	改变（进，良）	01
monitor	v.	检验（放射性污染）	03
moor	n.	荒野；沼	12
multiplication *	n.	增加，乘	05
multitude	n.	许多，大批（量）	07
a multitude of		许多的，众多的	07
municipal	a.	城市的	09
municipal solid waste		城市固体废物	14

municipality n. 市政当局，市政府		15
nationwide a. 全国性的		16
neither...is so easily...as... 都不能象……那样易于		06
nonuniform a. 不均匀的，变化的		10
nonuniform flow (=varied flow) 变速（不等紊）流		10
notably ad. 显著的，著名的		15
nutrient n. 养料，养分		02
nutrition n. 营养（学）		08
objectionable * a. 讨厌的，不适合的		05
obtainable * a. 能得到的，能达到的		06
odour n. 气味，臭味		05
option n. 选择，选择权		14
originate v. 发起，发生		13
ornate a. （装饰）华丽的		01
osmosis n. 渗透性		04
overweight v. 在重量上超过		14
outbreak n. 爆发，破裂		07
outrage n. 义愤，痛恨		11
outstrip v. 超越，胜过		03
oxidation n. 氧化（作用）		08
oxidize v. （使）氧化		08
oxygen free environment 无氧环境		14
ozone 臭氧		05
particulate n. 粒子		02
particulate combustion products 颗粒燃烧物		14
patent v. 为……取得专利 n. 专利，专利品		01
pathogen n. 病原体，病菌		04
pathogenic a. 致病的，病原的		02
per capita 每人（口）		13
percolation n. 渗透		09
periodic * a. 定期的		05
permeability n. 渗透性，透气性		09
permeable a. 可渗透的		09
persistently ad. 不断地，坚持地		16
phenol n. （苯）酚，石炭酸		05
pipeline n. 管道（线），输送管		11
plumbing n. （自来水，卫生）管道（装置）室内给排水系统		07
pollutant n. 污染物质；散布污染物质者		13
pore n. 小孔		09
porous * a. 多孔的		06
porous formation 多孔岩层		06
pose v. 提出，造成，形成		14
portability n. 可饮用		05
p.p.m.=parts per million 百万分之（几）		05
precipitate * v. 降水，沉降		02
precipitation n. 沉降物（雨，水等）		02
predominantly * ad. 显著地		02
preform v. 预先形成		08
priority * n. 重点，优先		16
privatization n. 私有化		16
profile n. 轮廓，断面（图）		10
programmer * n. 规划，订计划者		16
proliferate v. 繁殖，繁衍		08
protozoa n. 原生动物		02
provide for 提供，作准备		06
purify v. 使纯净，使洁净		06
pyrolysis n. 热解作风，高温分解		14
pyrolysis furnace 干馏炉，热解炉		14
quantitative * a. 数量的，定量的		12
quest vi. 追求，探索		16
rainfall n. 降雨，降水，降雨量		06
range v. 延伸；探寻；涉及		11
raw material 原材料		14
rayon n. 人造丝		05
recharge v. 再装，再补充		06
recharge well 回灌井		13
recognizable a. 可认出的		09

recommendation n. 建议，劝告		03
recoverable a. 可重获的，可找到的		14
rectangular a. 矩（长方）形的		10
refill v. 在装（灌）满		06
remainder n. 剩余物		09
reside v. 住（留）；属于		13
resistivity * n. 电阻性		05
restrain… 制止……（干）		15
resulting a. 所引起（产生）的		10
retard v. 延迟，放慢，阻滞		10
retarded flow 滞流，减速流		10
reveal v. 泄露；显示		11
reverse v. 扭转		03
round n. 循环，周期		03
runoff n. 径流（量）		06
sanitary a. 卫生的,关于环境卫生的		11
sanitary properties 卫生系数（性能）		04
sanitary or storm drainage 生活用水或雨水的排放		07
sanitation n. （环境）卫生		01
Sanskrit n.; a. 梵文（的）		01
savannah n. 热带大草原		12
secretion n. 分泌液		05
sediment n. 沉积（物）		09
sedimentation n. 沉积（物），沉积作用		01
seep (into, in) vi. 渗入		02
segment * n. 部分，分布		13
self-sustaining a. 自给的，自足的		14
separated sewer (system) 分流制下水管（系统）		15
septic a. 引起腐烂的		15
septic tank 化粪池		15
service v.; n. 服（勤，业）务，设备（施）		07
settle v. 澄清，（使）沉淀		01
settle/settling out 沉淀出来		04
settling n. 沉淀		04
severity n. 严重性		13
sewage n. （阴沟等处的）污水，污物		11
sewer n. 阴沟，污水管，排水管，下水道		11
sewerage n. 下水道，污水（排水）工程（系统）		10
shear force 切力		10
silica * n. 二氧化硅		05
siphon n.; v. 虹吸（管），用虹吸管输送		01
sodium * n. 钠		09
solid refuse 固体废物		13
sparsely ad. 稀疏地，稀少地		13
spatial a. 空间的		12
specialize v. 使专门化，特殊化		08
speculation n. 推测		01
spillway n. 溢洪（泄水）道		10
starch n. 淀粉		05
status n. 情形，状况		07
step by step 逐步，逐渐		08
sterilize v. 消毒，杀菌		04
still n. 蒸馏（器）		10
storage reservoir 蓄水库（池）		06
subdivide v. 细分		09
submerged a. 水面下的		07
substrate n. 基质，底质		09
superimpose v. 添加，附上		03
supervision n. 监控，检查，管理		14
supply source 水源		06
suspend water 悬着水		09
suspension * n. 悬浮(液),悬胶(体)		05
sustainable a. 持续的，能忍受的		16
synthesize v. （人工）合成		08
taper * v. 弄尖,（使）逐渐变细		01
tar a. 焦油，柏油		14
terminal community 最终群落		12
terrestrial a. 陆地的		12
tertiary a. 第三级的		15

the fire department 消防部门		06
toxic *a.* 有毒的，中毒的		02
toxicity *n.* 毒性，毒力		09
trace *n.* 痕量，微量		03
trace metals 微量金属		03
transparency *n.* 透明（性，度）		05
transpire *v.* 蒸发，气化		09
treat *v.* 讨论，探讨		10
treatise *n.* （专题）论文		01
trench *n.* 沟，渠		10
tributary *a.* 附属的，（河）支流的		11
turbid *a.* 混浊的		04
turbidity *n.* 混浊度		01
turbulent *a.* 湍（紊）流的		10
typhoid *n.* 伤寒		03
underlying * *a.* 根本的，基础的		16
undertaker *n.* 承担者，承办人		16
undesirable * *a.* 讨厌的，令人不快的		15
unrelenting *a.* 不退让的，不松懈的		13
unsaturated *a.* 未饱和的		09
unsuspected *a.* 未知的		05
uphill *n.* ; *a.* ; *ad.* 上坡，向上		07
urbanization *n.* 都市化		03
valve *n.* 阀门，开关		07
vent *n.* ;*v.* 通风(排气),管(口);		07
versatility *n.* 多面性，多功能性，变化性		08
voussoir *n.* （楔形）拱石,(拱)楔块		01
waste disposal 废物处理		15
watershed *n.* 流域；集水区		11
water-supply 给水的		06
water (supply) engineer 给水工程师		06
water undertaker 自来水厂		16
wedge *n.* 楔块，楔形物		01
wholesome *a.* 有益于健康的，卫生的		04
wick *n.* 灯心，(吸)油绳		01
Zuider Zee dam （荷兰)须德海堤坝		04

Appendix Ⅱ　　Translation for Reference

第 1 单元

供 水 历 史

人类在史前时期就开始寻求洁净的水。人类最早的许多活动是不难推测的。一些人可能在地上挖沟，把水引到所需要的地方，后来，空心圆木可能作为最初的水管得到使用。

一定是在数千年后，我们更近代的祖先才学会建设城市，享受到管道供水进家和下水道泄水排污的便利。有关集中给水排水设施的最早考古记录可上溯至约五千年前的苏米里亚的尼波城。在尼波城的废墟中有一拱顶下水道，其楔形石块尖头向下，被砌成完美的拱形。水由井和蓄水池汲入。完善的排水系统排除来自该城王宫和居民区的废水。

最早关于水处理知识的记载现保留在梵文医学典籍和埃及壁刻中。约公元前 2000 年的梵文著作叙述了如何通过在铜器皿中煮沸，日光照晒，木炭过滤和在陶土器皿中冷却等方法来净化污浊的水。

人们已知最早的液体净化装置出现在公元前 15 和 13 世纪的埃及壁画中，一幅画描绘了如何用虹吸管吸水或者是沉淀过的酒。另一幅画显示在当时埃及的厨房里使用油绳虹吸的方法。

公元 98 年，罗马水务长官赛克特斯·朱利叶斯·弗朗提纳斯作出了第一份有关供水和水处理的工程报告。他写了二本有关罗马供水的书。在这两本书中，他描述了位于一渡槽头的沉淀池。他的著作最先由著名的水利工程师克莱蒙斯·荷思切尔于 1899 年译成英文。

公元八世纪，阿拉伯炼丹术士詹伯写了一篇颇具专业水平的有关蒸馏的论文，其中涉及到水和其它液体的各种蒸馏器具。

英国哲学家弗朗西斯·培根爵士写到过他用过滤、煮沸、蒸馏和絮凝澄清等方法净化水的试验。有关试验情况于 1927 年即他死后一年发表。培根还指出澄清的水往往有益健康，令人"悦目"。

已知的第一个对砂滤池有插图的描述，由一位意大利的内科医生鲁克·安东尼奥·帕罗发表于 1685 年。他根据自己在奥土战争中的经历，写了一本关于军营中士兵保健的书。这很可能是有关公共卫生的最早的出版物。他描述并图示了砂滤池和沉淀法的使用。帕罗还指出他的过滤法与那些在威尼斯道吉宫和罗马卡帝诺·萨切特宫筑井的人使用的方法原理是一样的。

最古老的在考古学上已知的水过滤的例子见于威尼斯及其占领的殖民地。蓄水池华丽的池口上载有日期，但人们尚不知过滤池建于何时。威尼斯这个建在诸岛上的城市，一千三百多年以来靠接蓄雨水作为该市的主要淡水供应。人们建造蓄水池并把很多蓄水池和砂滤池相接。雨水自屋顶冲刷而下流至街道，在那儿被收集到有石格栅的集水池中，然后经砂床过滤至蓄水池。

关于威尼斯供水的一篇综述见于1863年的"实用力学期刊"。威尼斯陆地面积12.85英亩，年平均降雨量为32英寸。几乎所有的这些降雨都被收集在177个公共的和1 900个私人的蓄水池中。这些蓄水池日平均供水量约每人每天4.2加仑（qpcd）。如此低的耗水量部分归于缺乏下水道以及人们惯于在废水池洗衣服和普遍饮酒。在大约16世纪前，这些蓄水池一直是威尼斯的主要供水设备。

18至19世纪在英、法、德、俄等国做了许多试验。亨利·达西于1856年在法国和英国取得了滤池的专利，除絮凝工艺外，他在其它各方面促进了美国快速砂滤池的问世。他似乎首先将水力学原理应用于滤池设计。第一个供应全城镇用水的滤池于1804年建于苏格兰的佩斯里，但水是用车送至用户的。到1807年，在苏格兰的格拉斯哥，滤后水由管道输往用户。

在美国，直到内战之后水处理问题才得一顾。解决水混浊的问题不象在欧洲那样迫切。第一批滤池属慢速砂滤型，和英国的设计相似。约在1890年，快速砂滤池在美国问世，并使用了絮凝剂以提高滤池的效率。这些滤池经稍许改进，不久便发展成我们目前使用的快速砂滤池。

第2单元

水

动植物生存必须有丰富的、不含有毒物质和致病菌的水源。人类越来越向大城市集中，提供充足的洁净水这一问题也越来越重要。环卫工程师的一个主要职能便是保证清洁饮用水的供应。这一工作做得很出色，发达国家已能获得清洁、可靠的饮用水。这些国家的公民已习惯于饮用洁净水，而一旦到了国外的许多地方，他们就很容易成为污染水源的受害者。

水源

所有的水都来自降水。太阳热量从海洋、湖泊上蒸发了大量的水，同时也从地面上和动植物体内蒸发了大量的水，形成水蒸气上升，在空中形成浮云。浮云飘近山脉时被迫上升，升得越高，气温降得越低，使越来越多的水蒸气凝结。这样，浮云中的微粒逐渐变大，直到大得以降雨形式落到地面。

当水以雨、雪、雨夹雪和冰雹形式出现时，作用很像真空吸尘器，夹带走空气中的所有尘埃污物。当然，最初的降水所含的污染物的浓度最大，短暂时间以后，降水中的微生物就比较少了。水落到地面后，一部分流经地面，一部分渗入地下。

地面水

流经地面的水称作地面水。它在流回海洋途中夹带了微生物，有机物和无机物等许多物质。积聚在低洼处的地面水形成湖泊池塘，因为水中富含养分，成为各种微生物生长繁殖的理想场所。地面水中含有各种形态的微生物，其种类和数量直接反映了水的质量。

如果水中不含矿物质，几乎没有什么生物可以在水中生存。当较多的有机物和无机物进入地面水中，细菌，藻类和原生动物便生长繁殖起来。相当洁净的水中微生物含量很少，但种类较多。水中的污染物愈多，微生物的数量愈多，种类却随之减少。无机物含量较高的水中藻类生长茂盛，而有机物含量高的水中，细菌繁殖明显增加。微生物含量高的地面水在使用之前必须经过处理。"预防所用的一盎司抵得上救治所用的一磅"，人们正努力保护地面水库免遭污染，以避免进行大范围的水处理。

地下水

渗入地下的水称作地下水。当水流经地层表面时，带走一些液态的无机物和有机物，微生物和颗粒物质也在地层上部被滤出。因此，大部分地底深处的水不含微生物，水中无机物和有机物污染较少，当然，比地面水更宜于作饮用水源。

第3单元

水 质 问 题

落到地面的水中一部分被太阳蒸发，一部分渗入地层，可能被干渴的植物吸收，也可能汇入井水或泉水。大部分水则流回江河和海洋，重新开始这一过程。这就是"水循环"。

现代人生活的环境是复杂的演变过程的结果，这一过程在生命的起源时即开始。如果没有水，就不会发展到今天这样。所有的生物必须有水才能生存。无论是稀少的降雨之后短暂地发芽、开花的沙漠植物，还是主要依赖水来解渴和生产食物的人类本身都是如此。当我们探讨人类在为其自身创造的环境中的种种需求时，水质问题的严重性达到令人惊异的程度。

原始人在其进化过程中很早就意识到水对生存的不可缺性：人需饮水，而供食用的动植物也只在有充足的水源的地方才繁茂和兴旺。他们发现水可以用来抵御敌人的侵犯，又是一种很好的能源，同时也发现过多的水会引起泛滥和灾害。在现代，埃塞俄比亚干旱所带来的恐慌，孟加拉国水灾的严重后果都生动地说明水在环境中的重要地位。

几千年来，人类已意识到人对水的需求应当适量。但是随着技术的发展，都市的兴起，环境开始被污染，人们逐渐明白需要保证水的质量。不幸的是，在世界上工业化的社会里，贪婪和技术已超越了自然科学的发展。这导致许多河道遭受城市和工业废物的严重污染，也使沿河饮用这些水的市民和村民们，因为缺乏知识，缺乏监测和控制环境水质的设备，便面临着水传播的流行病的威胁，和过量的微量元素的威胁。

细菌学在19世纪中叶才得到完全认可，这充分说明当时人们知识的缺乏。然而在其后的几十年里，人们继续从排放污物的下游河道中取水供应，这些水没有经过或很少经过处理。每年伤寒和霍乱的循环发作曾经是生和死的常规特征。发达国家采用仔细选择水源和进行水处理的方式来控制水质，事实上已杜绝了水传播的流行病。这在第三世界却仍然是个问题。

通过我们现在才关注的环境中所含的过量的铅表明当时人们缺乏必要的检测仪器。只是在最近20～30年，才有了可靠的仪器精确地测出微量的铅（以及其它微量元素），更为重要的是评估出铅对人体的有害影响。

今天人类似已认识到自己在利用水源过程中的许多错误。他们正在制定各种标准，提出建议和准则以便在水循环的各个阶段中控制水质，以扭转在发达国家曾达到灾难性程度的污染趋势。

在水循环中，我们所关注的淡水部分只占3%。通常正是这3%的淡水用于维持健康、食物供应（农业和淡水渔业）、工业和消闲。因此，测量、监测和控制这一部分循环水的质量对所有的社会都是重要的。

当我们详细考虑如何着手时，重要的是要考虑自然界中什么影响了水质（自然界的污染），而人类又给它添加了什么（人为的污染）。

第4单元

水 的 净 化

只要把溶解其中的盐分去除，海水便可以作饮用水源。最直接的方法是蒸馏法：把水变为蒸汽然后凝结成水。过去，蒸馏法的代价一直很高，但在最近几年里，人们在降低蒸馏工艺成本方面已取得许多进展，想出许多巧妙的方法来解决这一问题。

另一种脱盐方法是电渗析。这是当水稍含盐分时最有效的电化学方法。这种水虽然也含盐，但含盐度没有海水那么高，例如可以在海水和河水交汇处的河口上游一段距离发现这种水。第三种用冰冻法来脱盐，因为冰接近纯净。第四种则靠高压，称为反渗透。

回到河流的话题上。人们常谈论用拦河坝来利用水源。在河口筑坝，从而在坝后形成淡水湖。如荷兰的须德海堤坝。

既然明白水传播的疾病会引起传染病流行，为防止传染，要组织供水系统。也就是说对水进行处理，不断地检测水质，以确信这些措施的有效性和效果的稳定性。处理水的基本目的是消毒（杀死其中可能含有的带病菌的有机物）。但是法律要求更为严格，它要求所有承担供水的公司（或市政管理部门）提供卫生的供水。这并非简单的要求"无害的"的水，而是要提供"有益于健康"的水。因此，为提高水质，可能要改变水的化学成分。

水处理的首要原则是先使水达到最大可能的纯净度，然后使之达到饮用标准。

有以下几个理由需对正常的供水作净化处理：首先是水的混浊。混浊的水中悬浮着固体的微粒，看上去不清澈透明。其次是水的颜色，颜色与浑浊并不是一码事。清洁水也可有颜色，如铁盐溶解其中。但卫生的水应当是无色的。净化还应包括去除味道、气味，还可能要去除水中生长的藻类——尤其是水库中的藻类。

然而最重要的是使水免遭污水的污染，或者使水不含病原体——那些带来疾病的生物。这需通过测定确保水中不含某些细菌。

把污水变成可饮用水的处理过程常包括以下步骤：

沉淀，使用或不使用化学絮凝剂都可导致粗大的颗粒下沉，以带走细菌和类似的更小颗粒。

然后可以让水通过相当厚的砂滤层，絮体被砂粒截留，形成更有效的过滤，能滤去大多数有机微粒和细菌。

过滤后的水，其水质和外观都已大为改善，卫生属性也大大提高，但往往不能完全去除细菌。因此常用氯来消毒。

第 5 单元

水分析的基本指标

颜色

颜色是由于溶解或悬浮在水中的胶体有机物的存在而产生的。颜色与有机物的数量无关，因为有机物可能有色也可能无色。

有色的水若用于家庭生活，尤其用于饮用是令人不愉快的。因为这种水究竟能否饮用总是引起疑问。某些工业要求其用水完全无色，因为颜色可能影响所加工的产品，从而降低其质量；造纸、人造丝、纤维素、淀粉以及印染等工业就是例证。

除去水的颜色要靠混凝作用。

臭与味

臭和味通常是由诸如藻类和真菌等生活在水中的生物所排泄的分沁物所引起的。某些化学药品，即使剂量小，也会放出难闻的气味。苯酚就是这样。它与氯化合形成恶臭的氯酚。从健康的角度来看，令人不快的味道不很重要。然而在饮水中有这些味道却是极其令人讨厌的。

这种令人讨厌的味道可用折点加氯法、活性炭、二氧化氯以及臭氧等去除。所有的水样，无论取自什么水源，都会由于溶解了各种盐类和各种气体而具有各自独特的味道。

浑浊度

浑浊度表明水中悬浮物的含量。

我们可以利用二氧化硅，将其透明程度与加上二氧化硅的人工配制的悬浮液进行比较，来表示水的浑浊度。浑浊度表示将分别在不同的时间最终沉淀下来的细微的悬浮物质的浓度。这些悬浮物是粘土、细砂、石灰石微粒等等。用滴入胶粘剂来测量浑浊度的办法在确定不可沉淀和不能被滤除的那些胶质微粒的含量方面特别有用。这就是之所以在通过滤纸对液体进行过滤，排除了粗大颗粒的影响之后，还有必要进行上述测试的原因。同时，这样做也是为了确切地知道那些通常产生颜色的胶状物质所导致的混浊程度。

饮用水的浑浊总是令人不愉快的。

含有可能最终沉淀的悬浮物质的水，由于会在管道和储水池里形成沉积，所以总是造成麻烦。

最后，在制品需要与水接触的工业中，总是要求清亮的水，同时常常允许有某种胶体混浊度。

浑浊度与透明度有关。

小于10滴胶粘剂的浑浊度值表示深度达4米的良好透明度。可是饮用水通常要求小于4滴胶粘剂的浑浊度值。

只有通过凝聚作用才能去除胶体浑浊度。

通常，水是在具有或不具有凝聚作用的沉淀池中澄清，然后再过滤的。

若水中所含的悬浮物不到20p.p.m.，而这些悬浮物又可通过使用不多于20p.p.m.的絮凝剂来凝聚和去色的话，这样的水就可以用直接过滤法来进行处理。

对于浑浊度的了解是进行水处理的一项不可缺少的要素。

导电性与电阻性

导电性取决于所溶解的固体的浓度。导电性的测定是件相当容易的事情。它能告诉我们水中的盐浓度。了解盐浓度对于定期检验某一给定的水来说是特别有用的，因为这样就可以直接得知水成分的变化情况。

温度

不可能用任何处理方法来控制给水工程的水温，在此意义上，水温检验并无实际意义。从蓄水库供给的水，其温度取决于取水的深度。要求饮用水的温度为10℃，而25℃被认为是不适合的。

然而，应该注意到，水从水源到干管的温度变化有助于发现未知的污染源。并且，细菌在高温水中的增长速度较之低温水中更加迅速。因此，当15℃左右的水被收集来作细菌分析时，就必须尽快地冷却下来。此外，还必须记住，提取水样时的温度应该随时记录下来。

pH 值

pH 值能说明水究竟是酸性还是碱性。pH 值小于7倾向酸性，而pH 值大于7则倾向碱性。

pH 值的大小与健康无关，然而在决定水的腐蚀作用时，pH 值却是一个很重要的因素。

定期地测量 pH 值是水处理实践中必不可少的一环。尤其在絮凝过程的效率方面，它起着重要的作用。

第 6 单元

给 水 工 程

城市给水系统通常包括一个位于水源处的蓄水库，从蓄水库到城市附近的配水库的管道以及埋设在街道下面的将水送入住户、商店、工厂和机关的配水管。因此，给水工程的主要设备就是两座水库，及其间的管道网。蓄水库的作用是储足一年或数年的用水量，以保证干旱期间全部高峰用水量。配水库的作用则是保证一天或一星期的用水量。由于有了蓄水库，给水水源可以小些，费用也少些；同样，由于有了配水库，管道和水泵都可以比没有配水库时小些，因而也便宜些。

美国某些城市的用水量按人口平均计在全世界是最高的。每人的用水量变化于 200—5 000 升/日之间，平均约为 500 升/人·日。但是不能认为气候较冷的国家的用水量最后也要达到同样的用水水平，因为美国所需的最高用水量大多是由于夏季空调设备以及花园浇水方面所耗用的。

给水工程师必须研究所在地区的人均用水量（每人耗用的水量），并根据那里最先进的社区的用水量选定一个数值，所确定的人均用水量必须乘以自计划供水期往后 30 年或 30 年以后的估计人口数。由于供水和储水设施都不能象配水系统那样易于扩建，所以它们都必须设计得有足够的容量，以满足这一时期的需要。而配水系统则可随供水需求的增长及住宅的建设而扩展。

一旦计算出每年所需的供水量，并经包括消防部门在内的所有有关方面同意后，则确保能够真正永久地从所建议采用的集水处取得所需供水量就成为重要的问题。所谓集水处是将水泄入供水水源的区域。每年泄入水库的水量不可能超过该流域的降雨量，而且通常还要比之小得多。

给水水量通常可以从地表水（雨水）或地下水取水，或二者兼得。地表水和地下水均由雨水补给。地表水由地面径流补给。而泉水与井水则由进入地下的水，即渗透水补给，这两部分水量，加上蒸发水及树木和其它植物所吸收的水，组成总降雨量。即使城市给水包括该区域内的全部泉水及地表水，但由于水的蒸发和植物生长的需要，仍然不可能取得全部降雨量。

因此，把降雨量记录、径流量和渗透率，同河流流量记录及当地其它水文资料加以核对，是非常重要的。渗透水，即渗入地下变成地下水的雨水，能在地下作长距离的水平流动，可以流入或者流出集水区。如果每年的供水量超过每年的降雨量，地下水位一般将下降，其结果是不能获得所需要的供水量。这时必须寻找别的水源。

如果能将水储存在地下，就没有必要建造水库或蓄水池，而把水储存于地下往往是可能的。事实上，在伦敦地区，由于抽水的缘故，该地区白垩土层内的水位一个多世纪以来一直在不断下降。因此有人建议，今后不再使用一直沿用到现在的地面蓄水库蓄水，而改为向井内回灌净水以补充白垩土层内的水量而达到蓄水的目的。

这种地下储存的方法，目前正广泛地为许多国家的煤气工业所采用。在供气量多时，用压缩机通过井把煤气送入地下密封的砂层、石灰岩层或其它多孔岩层中储存，以供需气量大于供气量时之用。这种地下储气库往往比现有最大的储气罐大几百倍，已公认为是一种实用价廉而安全可靠的储气方法。

第 7 单元

室内管道工程
——背景与现状

  为保护人类健康,并为人们提供较舒适的生活方式而发展起来的最重要的系统之一就是室内管道系统,该系统就是用管道向用户输送饮用水,并将废物排入各种处理流程进行处理。在现代社会中,我们必须认识到:室内管道系统对于社会犹如循环系统对于人体那样重要。为了避免传染病的爆发和化学污染,室内管道系统必须有效地进行工作。在住宅区内,良好的卫生设施要求室内管道系统应当没有交叉连接、倒流连接、配水出口淹没以及通风不良等现象,还应当向现代社会提供充足的优质饮用水。当今社会面临的最大困难之一在于:现存的较陈旧的管道系统可能逐渐损坏、并将给人们健康带来危害。同时,室内管道系统的维修方式也可能直接危害健康。

  室内管道工程是指对饮水供应系统、生活用水或雨水排放系统及通风系统中的管道、装置、设备以及附件进行安装、维修、更换等作业及所使用、材料和装置。但它并不包括钻井、水软化设备的安装以及卫生用具、设备、器具和零件的制造或销售。室内管道系统是由充足的饮用水供给系统、安全充足的排水系统、足够的器具及设备所组成。

  长期以来,公共卫生人员对室内管道系统及公共饮用水配水系统中的交叉连接、倒流连接和进水口淹没等问题一直很关注。这些交叉连接可能使饮用水受到非饮用水或污水的污染。虽然饮用水受污染的可能性似乎很小,但诸多问题确实存在。唯一可行的预防措施就是不采用可能使饮水遭污染的连接和渠道。当安装管道人员没有意识到这种危险性、不懂得水会倒流时,就会出现交叉连接。事实上水甚至可以向上流动。此外阀门有可能失灵或由于大意使其开启着。为了同这一污染问题作斗争,安装人员必须懂得水力学及其引起环境卫生公害的各种污染因素。他们还必须知道可采用哪些合格的装置和方法以防止倒流以及如何获得这些材料并适当地安装起来。

  本文的目的并非对室内管道系统作全面介绍,更不是列出所有的潜在危害,而是给环卫专业人员提供充分的素材和图表以帮助他们更好地了解室内管道系统及其与人体健康的关系。

  由于在这一领域缺乏资料,故很难弄清室内管道系统目前存在的问题。然而,可以肯定:由于年代已久,许多地区的室内管道系统正趋破损。不幸的是,有关近75年以来室内管道系统的唯一新事物则是仅仅采用了塑料管道。由于在这方面进展缓慢,许多人对可能导致疾病或危害的微生物的、化学的或物理的诸因素的巨大的潜在威胁未能给予足够的重视。

第8单元

微生物的化学机理

1857年，路易·巴斯德发表了一篇报告，指出牛奶变酸是由于微生物造成的，它们将牛奶中的糖变成了乳酸。这一反应可用化学式表达如下：

$$C_6H_{12}O_6 \longrightarrow 2CH_3CHOHCOOH$$
$$(糖) \qquad\qquad (乳酸)$$

从这一反应的总结果，至少从表面上看，这是可以想象的最为简单的化学变化之一，它实际上表示一个糖分子分解成为两个乳酸分子。

现在我们来看巴斯德在同一时期所研究的糖的另一种转换，即酒精发酵，葡萄汁转化为葡萄酒便是这一转变的一个例证。在这一例子中，正如众所周知的那样，造成这一变化的微生物是酵母菌，它把葡萄汁中的糖转换为酒精，其反应式如下：

$$C_6H_{12}O_6 \longrightarrow 2CH_3CH_2OH + 2CO_2$$
$$(糖) \qquad (酒精)$$

有氧或无氧

葡萄酒被暴露于空气中会变成醋，而这正是巴斯德所论述的下一个问题。他指出在这一例子中，造成变化的是另一种微生物，这些微生物使酒精氧化为醋酸，其化学式如下：

$$CH_3CH_2OH + O_2 \longrightarrow CH_3COOH + H_2O$$
$$(酒精) \qquad\qquad (醋酸)$$

正如我们刚才所了解的那样，糖转变为乳酸或酒精都与氧气的存在无关，而酒精变为醋酸却是由于空气中的氧参与的一种氧化作用造成的。与此相反，巴斯德观察到当一种糖溶液被置于一个氧气被完全除去的环境中时，就可能出现一种完全不同的物质，即丁酸。在这些条件下，繁殖的细菌在无氧状态下得以最佳生存，而且事实上，它们在有氧气的环境中可能会死亡。"厌氧"细菌（沿用巴斯德本人的说法）把糖转化为丁酸，是按照下面这一简略的化学式进行的，这与"厌氧"发酵是相符合的，也就是说，这一发酵不涉及到氧气的利用：

$$C_6H_{12}O_6 \longrightarrow CH_3CH_2CH_2COOH$$
$$(糖) \qquad\qquad (丁酸)$$

微生物世界

我已列举了四种不同类型的化学变化过程，不仅是为了表明巴斯德对微生物化学所作出的贡献，而且更为了说明微生物在化学方面的多功能性。从这些简单的例子中所应学习的一个重要课程就是，任意给定一种物质，它都可被转变为多种不同的衍生物，这取决于该物质受到何种类型的微生物的作用以及该作用所发生的特殊条件。

巴斯德发现，每一种微生物都或多或少地专门引起几种化学反应。对于每一种有机物来说，自然界中至少存在一种，通常有数种在适合的环境下能够将其腐蚀和分解的微生物。这些各种类型的微生物在自然界中几乎无所不在，它们将所有的复合有机物逐步分解为越来越单一的化合物。微生物是将生命与物质以及物质与生命维系在一起的无穷无尽的循环链中必不可少的链节。没有它们，生命便会即刻消亡。

微生物在自然界中所起的巨大作用的又一证据就是：根据最近的统计，地球上微生物的总质量大约为动物的总质量的二十倍。

近几十年中，研究微生物营养学的科学家们发现，维生素为证明从最大的到最小的不同形态的生命之间的相似性提供了进一步的证据。实际上，许多微生物可以在一些维生素含量不足以满足动物和人的生存和生长的培养基中繁殖。然而究其原因，这些微生物自身可以将较简单的物质合成为维生素，从而制造出足够的维生素来满足其自身的需求。换言之，无论微生物的繁殖是否需要预先形成的维生素，它们都会使用与动植物及人大致相同的方法，利用这些物质来进行其生物化学活动。

第9单元

地下水的形成与运动

除了地表淡水系统之外，工业，家用和农业的另一类重要的水源是地下水。近期数据表明，美国大陆每日所用地下水高达810亿加仑以上，这占了美国全部用水量的20%，其中每天有420亿加仑用于农业灌溉，310亿加仑用于农村地区，80亿加仑用于城市和工业，这些地下水来源于在水未饱和地层以下流动的并进入地下水位的那部分雨水和雪水。

进入地下的一部分水将会被岩石，土壤截留并作为悬着水保持在上层土壤中。来自周围土壤颗粒的和水分子相互间存在的分子吸力防止悬着水流入更深的土壤中。因为在这一区域中，土壤颗粒之间的空间充满空气和水的混合物，所以这部分土壤叫做通气层，并且它还可细分为不同的三层：湿土层，中间层（可能存在也可能不存在）和毛细管作用层。

进入湿土层的水，一部分可能被蒸发或蒸腾，余下的部分则进入中间层，由于分子吸力，它常作为悬着水保持在这里。在中间层中，除了在降雨期间又有水加入外，几乎没有水的流动。有些地方没有中间层，湿土层直接处于第三层——毛细管作用层之上。水由于毛细管的作用而从下面流入毛细管作用层。

水饱和层位于通气层的下面，这一层没有残留的空气，土壤中的孔隙完全被地下水所饱和，饱和层和通气层之间的界面称为地下水位。它被定义为地下水在重力作用下流进水井的那个水位。地下水的储量，深度及流动的程度由土壤及下层土的结构所控制。大多数土壤和下层土都是由岩石和岩石碎片组成，其颗粒大小，密度和压实程度各不相同。有些土壤颗粒可能很小，形状规则，这就导致了颗粒间的密切"嵌合"，几乎没有孔隙，由于孔隙程度低，这些下层土在颗粒间不可能保持太多的水，所以说，它的渗透性低，换句话说，这种性质的下层土的持水性和导流能力差。粘土就是这种土的一个例子。另一些下层土可能由形状不规则的大颗粒组成，颗粒之间粘合性差，这类结构会导致许多小而相互连接的孔隙，水可以流入这些孔隙并在孔隙中流动。这类下层土的持水性和导流性强。因此它是有渗透性的土层。砾石或砾性下层土是渗水性能高的材料，公认为具有渗透性，同时水可以通过它流动的那些下层土被称为含水层。

在地下水位以下，即在水饱和区内，由于渗透作用，地下水经常会通过相互连接的孔隙而流动。在重力作用下，地下水从高水位区域流向低水位区域。地下水是由雨水和融雪水渗入土壤而得到补充的。因为降雨量和渗透性能的差异，所以渗透速率不均匀，这就导致了地下水位高低不匀，在高降雨量（或高渗透性）地区，地下水位高，在低降雨量（或低渗透性）地区，地下水位低，这种不均匀分布引起了地下水处于永恒的运动中。因为重力的作用，地下水便从高水位（高水头）区域流向较低水头（低水位）区域。通常，地下水倾向于流向地面江河和池塘。地下水流的速率由含水层的渗透性和该系统中的水头决定。地下水的流动速度等于水力梯度（单位长度上的水压差）乘以渗透系数，该系数表示底层允许水流通过的程度。如果已知流速，就可以计算出通过沉积物的水流容积（导水率）。地下水流的速度和方向通常用以下方法确定：把染色液投入回灌井中并监测相邻的试验井，直到染色液到达试验井为止。当水中溶解物质干扰染料探测时，可用向回灌井中投放氯化钠并监测相邻的试验井的方法，直到探测出氯离子为止。

地下水与地表水比较起来流动得较为缓慢，在深含水层中的流速从每日0.5厘米以下到每日约100厘米不等。在大多数含水层中，地下水只以每日几厘米的速度流动，但是在接近地面的渗透性良好的土壤和下层土中，地下水流速可高达每日15厘米。

第10单元

明 渠 流

明渠流是指渠道中流体部分界面暴露在大气压下的流体运动。这种渠道可以敞开在大气中，如天然河床、人工运河以及沟渠；也可以是封闭的，如非满流的排水管。

明渠流有别于被环绕的固体界面完全封闭的液体管流，也不同于完全被大气环绕的（流体）自由射流。管道的固体界面能够承受其表面的各种不同的压力。然而明渠流的自由表面的存在确保暴露于大气中的界面压力恒定不变。

等截面管道摩擦流动必须有压差来维持流动；横截面不变的明渠摩擦流动则是靠地球引力的影响，即渠道高度的变化来维持。与管流不同的是，明渠流的过水断面能够随着不同的流动状况而改变，且受制于渠道的界限。例如，通过矩形断面明渠的流动，液体深度的变化会形成不同的矩形过水断面。

正如管流一样，明渠流的性质可能是层流，也可能是紊流。当液体是水的时候，最为常见的是紊流。在测定和控制河水流动以及确定灌渠设计要求时，对明渠流进行分析是重要的。

本章将运用在前几章中获得的方法和液流基本方程对明渠恒定流的各个方面加以探讨。

首先，将要给出和明渠流有关的几个定义。当过水断面沿着流动方向不变时，这种流动称之为均匀流；反之则称为非均匀流。因此在明渠均匀流中，液体的深度是不变的，液体的表面与渠底是平行的。当液体的深度变化时，就会形成明渠非均匀流（也称之为变速流）。当渠道断面的形状或渠底的形状改变时，就会产生这一种流动。如果下游方向的深度增大，流速会减慢，而形成滞流；如果下游方向的深度减小，速度则增加，就会形成加速流。

在任何一个足够长的、坡度及断面保持不变的渠道里，都会形成均匀流动。下面给出一个均匀流如何形成的例子。图10-1所示为某一坡度有变化的灌渠。由于渠流坡度有变化，沿流动方向的重力分量大于阻滞流动的渠壁的切力，故流动就会产生加速，随着流速增大，切力也相应增大，达到某一速度时，切力与重力分量相等。在这种平衡条件下，速度和液体的深度保持不变，流动则变成明渠均匀流。

从图10-1可以看出，渠底坡度的变化会形成明渠非均匀流。当一种障碍物，如溢洪道，建在能形成均匀流的倾斜渠道上时，就会形成渐变流。障碍物后水面所形成的轮廓被称为回水曲线。

第11单元

环境或卫生工程

环境或卫生工程涉及为城乡提供清洁安全的供水系统，它也涉及到通过下水道系统处置剩余水和废料。环境或卫生工程的许多方面都直接与水利工程有关。的确，我们在前一章已经讨论过的一些工程就是给水系统的组成部分。例如，向洛杉矶市供水的胡佛水坝，它通过一系列的穿过美国西南部沙漠和山岭的运河、隧道和高架管道与该市连接。

大量的考古资料已经显示给水系统在古代就很重要，大概给人印象最深刻的就是罗马人建造的一些系统，这些系统的输水渠道仍存在于现代的意大利、西班牙、法国和土耳其。罗马本身的供水量估计每日5 000万加仑，或城市的每个居民的日供水量为50加仑。水被输送到喷水池，人们从这儿用罐子取水，然后带回家，仅有少数建筑物和住宅有与输水干线接通的接户管。罗马还有一条下水道，叫作大下水道，其中一部分至今仍在使用。象古代其它下水道一样，该下水道原来是用于排除雨水或公共浴池的废水。往里面倾倒固体废物是要受到处罚的。

罗马帝国覆灭后，相对地说，供水和排水系统曾长期受到忽视。在中世纪的欧洲，人们从河流和水井中取水，而将废水排入污水池或者甚至返回到原来取水的河流中。直到十九世纪证实了给水与某些疾病（如伤寒）有联系以后，全世界的都市与城镇才建起了安全的供水系统，美国三座城市的经验暴露出在建造大型供水系统时的某些工程问题，以及经济和立法问题。

芝加哥在仅仅几十年内就从一个密执安湖畔的小商埠发展成一个很大的城市。从这个城市的最初期开始，就存在着向快速增长的人口供水的问题。最初的水源为靠近城市的湖泊，但湖水常常被芝加哥河所排出的水污染，该河在城市发展的初期就像个污水明渠。在暴雨和洪水之后，污染就特别严重，甚至将取水泵移到远离岸边的地方，也不能解决问题。最后决定使芝加哥河水倒流，这样它就不排入湖中而流入密西西比河的支流—伊利诺斯河。可是，当借助于芝加哥卫生航运运河完成了这一任务之后，芝加哥下游城市和城镇的居民由于供水水源被芝加哥的废水所污染而发出义愤的呼声，接着又提出诉讼。最后，该城被迫建了几个大型污水处理厂，在废水排入芝加哥河以前将有害物质除去。

纽约市曾不得不建造一个从相当远处将水输往该城的系统。随着该城的发展，必须从愈来愈远处寻找新的水源。当前，纽约的水多来自该城西北方向特拉华河的集水区，此河在哈得逊河对过，卡茨基尔山脉的那边，水穿过世界上最长的隧道—特拉华水渠被输送到该城的蓄水系统，水渠延伸169公里，大部分穿过基岩。在某些地点渠道埋深达750米。纽约供水系统每日供水约13亿加仑—该城每人每日供水远远超过100加仑。

洛杉矶位于少雨区，当该城人口开始迅速增长时，水引自350公里以外横贯沙漠和山脉的科罗拉多河。供应洛杉矶和加利福尼亚南部各区用水的科罗拉多河水渠有1 081公里长。一个正在施工的更有雄心的工程项目将从多雨的加利福尼亚北部向本州较干燥的中部和南部引水。

第12单元

生 态 系 统

生态系统可以是生物圈的一小部分或一大部分。它是群落生境（非动物环境）和生物群落（植物和动物的王国）的具有相互作用的统一体，有一定的物质和能量流动。

生物群落是一系列具有一定空间分布的生物，这种分布是由外界环境因素和生物种类之间的相互关系所决定的。森林，草地，荒野，沼泽，湖泊和海洋都是生态系统。在世界上不同地区，生物圈是由以下部分 即自然生态系统（落叶森林，亚热带的大草原等，这依赖于气候因素）、半耕作生态系统（草地和人工森林）和耕作生态系统（农田）组成。它具有的特性是由其特定的植物和动物群落所决定并形成动物栖息地和植物产地。正是生态系统的存在为地球上的生命和人类的生存提供了一个基础。

陆上的或水中的生态系统的功能是以下列四种成分为基础的：

1. 非生物环境（群落生境），即各种生态因素（空气，水和土壤）的组合。

2. 生产者（自养成份），是指具有叶绿体的绿色植物（树，灌木丛，草本植物，农作物，海生的和淡水的藻类），它们将太阳能转化为化学能。生产者从无机物中生产出有机物，并以碳水化合物，蛋白质和脂肪的形式积累有机物。仅在有适当数量的自养生物（即绿色植物）存在的情况下，生态系统才能被认为是"完全"的。目前，地球上的大部分地区都被自养生态系统覆盖着。生产者是食物链的起始点。一切生物的存在（包括人）都依赖于生产者的存在。生产者的总同化速率称作初级生产总量。初级生产总量包含同化产生的有机物总量，其中包括植物在其本身生命过程中所消耗的有机物的量。

3. 消耗者（宏观的和微观的消费者，非自养者）组成了具有下列成分的另一大类。

（a）第一类消耗者是由食草动物组成。它们是直接或初级消耗者。初级消耗者利用在绿色植物中积累起来的碳水化合物、蛋白质和脂肪并通过分解它们使潜在的植物能源可供动物在其他喂养过程中使用。

（b）间接的消耗者，即食腐动物，包括生活在水中和土壤中的无脊椎动物。

（c）食肉动物形成消耗者的"顶峰"。

此类消耗者的存在对生态系统而言并不是必不可少的。在耕地的生态系统中（如麦田）食草动物常以害虫的形式出现。它们的活动可通过综合的植物保护而得到某些减弱。在这种情况下，初级生产的消耗者就是人自身。

4. 腐败生物包括各种不同的微生物，细菌和真菌。间接消耗者和微生物在自然生态系统中起着非常重要的作用。它们的任务就是将死亡的有机物转换到食物循环系统中。分解者是自然，半耕作和耕作生态系统的基本成份。

在生态系统中，自身调节作用对于物种的自身维护是很重要的。为使其自身适应生物和非生物环境，物种的数目需要在一定量的限度内波动。生态缓冲系统（自身调节作用，内部调节作用）是相对稳定的生态系统的首要特征。由于物种组成的多样性，整个生物群落的适应性和相对稳定性是很大的。如今，具有自身调节作用的生态系统已很少存在，甚至它们表面上看起来没有被打破的平衡也正在消失，例如自然保护区的生态系统。

在演变的进程中，对于某一生物群落在一给定的地区内发育进化是需要一段时间的。经过几个阶段（每个阶段都分别与各自的生物群落和群落生境相对应）后，整个发展过程（多级）达到一个所谓的最终群落（极顶）。最终群落与气候条件达成平衡，它是稳定的，并相对恒定一段时间。在我们所面临的气候条件下，森林就是这样的最终群落。

生态系统在物种的保存方面起着重要作用。一些物种，特别是具有广阔的生态范围的物种常在不止一种生态系统中出现。在这些物种中，会涉及到多种群落生境和不同的生态类型。自然生态系统和半耕作生态系统的消失危及物种的遗传及生态的变异性。植物园中物种的收集仅能部分补偿遗传变异上的损失。

第13单元

大气污染形成的因素

虽然污染并不是一种新的现象，但现在，它显然是飞速恶化的环境问题之一，在大气环境最近趋于恶化的过程中起作用的因素是什么呢？主要有下列三大因素，可说明这个问题。

第一个因素是人口的增长问题，第二次世界大战以来，美国人口增长的趋势，的确令人难以忘怀。人口越多，就意味着制造的商品和提供的劳务也越多，这反过来又导致了第二个因素。

第二个因素是工业和技术的扩展。从现有工厂生产能力的扩大和新的制造加工企业数目的增加来看，同一时期工业活动的增加也同样引人注目。另外，还引进了大量的新工艺，新方法和新产品。由这些新技术的一部分所带来的空中废物的性质，直到在它们对人类及其环境的有害影响突然变得明显之后，人们对此才有所了解。最近几十年内大规模引进了新产业和新工艺，包括钢铁生产的氧矛切割，石油产品的催化裂解，共聚物的生产和原子能。在大多数情况下，人们最初并不知道其原料和副产品废料所具有的毒性；同时有关怎样缓和所产生污染问题的方法与步骤等方面的知识，也远远落后于制造加工技术。大量增加的空中排出物，包括特性不明的各种物质相互结合，又促使大气污染恶化与复杂化。

第三个因素是社会变化，在这同一时期发生了两种重要的社会变化，从而也加速了大气污染恶化的趋势。

1. 都市化

人们竭力从农村地区迁到都市中心居住已导致城市飞快地发展成为大都会。在美国东海岸，波士顿，纽约，费城，巴尔的摩和华盛顿等大城市面积的发展，已经导致整个地区实质上合并成一个大都会。在这些城市之间已不再有20年或更多年以前存在的人口稀少的开阔地区。几年内，全国四分之三以上的人口将居住在全国百分之一的土地面积上。而发展结果是人口、工商业活动密度不断增加。这样，空中污染物的制造者比以前更多，而又与可能的接受体很靠近。那样的并置极大地增加了两者相互影响的频率和严重性，极难达到使人们可以接受的大气环境的目标。

2. 近几年来间接促使大气污染强化的另一社会因素，是这段时期中人们生活水平的普遍提高。大部分人口在经济上已经能过上较好的生活，包括高质量的食品，住房，交通工具和种种省力装置。在今天，很少有家庭没有小汽车，电视机，电冰箱，自动洗衣机和干燥机等。这些巨大数量的设备大多需要电能，这又部分地说明了这一事实：在美国，电力的需求量每十年增加一倍。大多数电能都是由电厂烧煤或石油发出的。由于这些燃料的燃烧产生大量的污染物，由这个污染源所引起的大气污染的潜力正在快速增加。

每个美国家庭实际上都高度依赖的小汽车，也是另一个重要的污染源，其污染物从内燃机里大量排出。

在现代社会里，每个人所制造的固体垃圾比以往任何时候都多，更多地使用纸，塑料和类似的材料作专用容器以及食品和大量生活用品的包装，极其需要固体废物处理设施。各种类型，各种规模的露天燃烧和煅烧炉散发出的污染空气的燃烧产物，其数量与化学复杂性不断上升。

这样，为人们提供更舒适，方便的条件和省时省力的机器，极大地加重了由于提供所需电力的能量转化过程所产生的大气污染。这样，一个更为富裕，教育程度更高的社会要求有一个比这个国家过去曾经享有的更好的生活环境，但人们却未料到这正好间接地促进了人们所厌恶的环境恶化。

当今社会人口的增长，工业和技术的发展以及社会变化的联合影响，可以看作是近年来导致城市空气环境严重变质的复合因素。在某些大城市，例如纽约、洛杉矶、费城、芝加哥和圣路易斯，这种趋势已达到惊人的地步。在那些地区，污染速率经常超过了大气本身所具有的扩散稀释等自然净化能力。在这期间发生严重的空气污染，并从对人眼的刺激，大气能见度降低和其它有害影响中清楚地显露出来。

第14单元

固体废物处理

固体和危险废物在最终处置以前可先进行预处理或加工。废物的处理和加工有几个优点,首先,它可用来减少所需处置的废物的体积和重量;它也可改变废物的形式和改进废物的处理特性。例如,通过称之为堆肥的过程可使垃圾和其他有机废物变成无害的甚至是有用的物质。最后,加工过程能够用来回收废物中的自然资源和能量以便再循环和再使用。"废物"中的大部分实际上可被用作生产的原材料。然而,任何废物加工或回收系统的固有的基本缺点乃是建设及操作的额外费用。

减少固体的体积和重量的最有效的办法之一是在一个设计合理的炉子中,在适宜的温度和操作条件下燃烧。这个过程叫做焚化。焚化过程是昂贵的,并且除非提供适当的空气清洁装置,否则气体和颗粒燃烧物的排放将会造成空气污染。这一过程也需要高水平的技术管理和技术工人进行合理的操作和保养。

然而,焚化的优点常超过它的缺点。焚化能减少普通垃圾的总体积的80%以上。在人口稠密的城市区域,由于合理的运距内不可能提供一个很大的场地用于堆放垃圾,焚烧对于固体废物处理可能是唯一经济的选择。在某些情况下,合理的设计、操作焚化炉以便将燃烧所产生的热量回收并用于生产蒸气或发电也是可行的。焚烧也可以用来销毁某些类型的危险废物。

在城市固体废物(MSW)的焚烧中,回收和再利用热量从环境和生态观点来看是一个有吸引力的废物处理的选择。但正如已提及的问题,诸如设备及控制的高费用、熟练技术人员的需要、辅助燃料的需要,又使得这一方法缺少足够的吸引力。

没有热量回收的焚化过程管理则较简单,费用比回收系统少三分之一以上。然而,简单焚烧的结果的确将失去全部可回收的能量。由于公众的和政治的兴趣在"再循环"上,所以在未来的几年里,可能逐渐要将重点放在城市固体废物热回收系统的设计和建造上。不管有或没有热量回收系统,焚化对固体废物处理比土地掩埋法具有较大的"吸引力",因为要找到合适的掩埋固体废物的场地变得越来越困难了。

城市固体废物处理的另一种相对新的发展是通过热化学转化。这一过程称作热分解作用,也称作干馏。它不同于传统的焚化而是一个吸热过程。就是说,整个过程需要不断地补充热能。(焚化,从另一方面来说是放热过程,当氧化发生时释放出热量)。

热分解是一个高温过程(1 100℃或2 000°F),它在少氧或无氧的环境下发生,由燃烧天然气来起动这一过程,但如果气态的热解副产品的70%用来循环到气体燃烧炉中,那么,这一过程就成为自保持的。

热分解过程包括一系列复杂的化学反应,而不是燃烧。这些反应将固体废物中的有机的碳组分分解或转化成为潜在的有用的副产品。热分解也能大量地减少固体废物的体积。干馏气体、液体、固体的副产品包括甲烷、甲醇、焦油和木炭。它们具有可燃性，可用作燃料，或者它们还可用作其他合成化学产品的原材料。

热分解的最终产物的实际组成可能各不相同。这不仅依赖于操作过程的温度和压力，同时还依赖于固体废物的性质。如果将玻璃、金属和其它无机物首先与将要加入到热解炉中的固体物质分离，则副产品的质量将有很大的改善。虽然废物分离需要附加费用，但热分解过程作为一种有效的废物处理方法仍具有很大的潜力。除了减少废物体积和产生有用的副产品以外，热分解过程对空气质量造成的威胁要比焚烧少。

第15单元

水污染防治

有效的污染控制系统取决于综合考虑技术、经济、社会及美学等因素而制定出来的决策。有关的决策包括必须回答许多复杂的问题。例如，我们怎样供水、什么时候、向什么人、为什么目的、提供多少、具有何种水质的水？谁将受到限制而不准向水系中的哪一部分排入多少哪一类的废水？谁在什么条件、什么情况下被允许利用水体来处置废水？谁将付出高昂的费用来保护地面和地下水体？等等。

要求绝对清洁或绝对纯净水的那种极端的观点就象要求对水的污染不加控制一样是不可接受的，因为在实际思考问题时必须考虑技术和经济上的可行性。

有几种防治水污染的方法。第一，通过废水处理可使水再使用和具有好的水质；第二，颁布和实施各项政府法规来禁止和限制水体的污染；第三，开发一些技术来防止或限制天然污染物径流（例如，从农业区域排出的天然污染物径流）进入水体。

美国控制水污染的传统方法是将废水收集在污水管道系统中，并将其输送到废水处理厂，在处理厂将污水加以处理以便排入河流或再使用。

有两类污水管道系统：合流制系统和分流制系统。合流下水管道既输送经人们利用后污染了的水，又输送从住房、街道或大地排泄的受污染了的雨水。在分流制系统中，污水管道只输送生活污水，而大量的雨水径流则由雨水道输送。在旱季，合流下水道只输送正常的水量，这部分水量全部都送至污水处理厂。但在雨季时，合流下水道不得不输送相当多的水量，这些水量的一部分，其中包括不同数量未经处理的生活污水，常常会跨越污水处理厂直接排入受纳河流。在这种情况下，可以依靠稀释作用减少污染，但这是一种很讨厌的情况。

废水通常采用两种工艺过程进行处理，称为一级处理和二级处理。在一级处理中，固体物质从水中沉淀出来，然后沉淀池的出水通过氯化作用加以处理以杀灭致病细菌和降低臭味。虽然美国有30％的城市对生活污水只进行一级处理，但该工艺过程不能满足大多数用水的要求。在二级处理中，只要利用有机物中的细菌就能去除生活污水中90％以上的有机物。在该工艺过程中，沉淀池的出水受细菌作用，细菌会消耗污水中大量的有机物质。二级处理的最后工序是投氯以杀灭出水中90%以上的有害细菌。在很少数的一些地区，如著名的塔霍湖附近区域，废水要进行进一步的三级处理，包括进一步净化水的许多新的工艺过程。

在缺少下水道系统或污水处理厂的地区，可采用氧化塘或化粪池。化粪池接收并保存家庭废水，让污水中的细菌破坏有机物以便使较清洁的水流进渗滤场。氧化塘具有适当的水深及停留时间，在太阳光、藻类和氧的综合作用下，也可使水回复至水质相当于标准二级处理可能提供的水质程度。

第16单元

使给水系统尽善尽美

"尽善尽美"是人们不断追求，而又不能完全达到的目标。

向人们居住的社区供应象水这样重要而又宝贵的东西，从来都是一项重大的事业，其主要目标在于满足人们的需求。社会对这种需求的认识，规定了把承担这项极其重要的任务作为其本身工作职责的供应者及有关当局的行为方式。

历史上完成这个目标经历了三个阶段。每个阶段都与一定的社会经济及文化发展水平相适应。1）量的阶段，此阶段的主要任务仅仅是满足人们在生物物理方面的需求。2）质的阶段，除了生物物理方面的需求之外，还有心理、文化、美学方面的目标。3）追求完美的阶段，在质的阶段之上，还加上可持续的社会、经济、文化因素。

在这一演化过程中，人群最初仅仅是一些数字（供应人口的百分数），到质的阶段成了消费者，到追求完美阶段，才成为有支配权的合作者。

当前的世界给水事业给我们提供了上述三个阶段的例子。在世界上许多地区，给水系统人口覆盖率很低，提高覆盖率是首要任务，服务质量问题还提不到第一位，必须让位给数量以及卫生方面的问题。

另一方面，到处都有明显的迹象表明，属于后两个阶段之间的较高要求的问题正在显得越来越重要。

当今，消费者的觉醒是一个无可争辩的因素，它影响着企业策略的制订和现场操作的规划。例如：南非的自来水公司现在就非常认真地从消费者的利益出发来考虑问题。去年五月份，我们还了解到，由于神户大地震和对没有给消费者提供充分信息的批评，日本人的态度也有所改变。

在葡萄牙，过去20年来，可以观察到一个重大而又积极的演变。目前，77%的人口已连接到公共给水系统，到2000年，其目标为95%。

三年前发表的一份官方的全国性调查，根据一些简化了的准则，认为40%的给水人口享受到良好的服务，54%得到适当的服务，6%受到不好的服务。

给消费者提供的服务质量，从今以后，将成为根本性的问题，特别是在供水连续性、水质和可靠性等方面。

因此，对于葡萄牙的自来水工业，追求尽善尽美既是一个挑战，也是一项必须完成的使命。

今后若干年内，预期将有重大的资本投入，以便改善现有的服务水平，特别强调正确安排好轻重缓急的顺序，和发展一种新的企业文化，提高管理效率和消费者满意的水平。这就需要在全国范围内采取多种多样的措施，包括制定一个在今后几十年内可持续发展的协调一致的构想。

为达到这个目标而提出的若干倡议最近可望得到认可。将出台新的立法，实施国家的和欧洲的基金计划，开展旨在支持对给水设施进行技术管理方法的应用研究。

在全国范围内评估服务水平的做法并不多见。英格兰和威尔士也许是目前最好的范例。从他们的经验中可以学到许多东西。但是，我们葡萄牙的情况和其他国家有根本的区别。我国的给水设施主要由地方当局管理，其组织框架与别的国家有所不同。一般来说，自来水厂规模较小，技术水平和财政能力都较低。给水和污水处理设施的全盘私有化也是一个不能低估的关键因素。

需要引进一整套新概念，以便把服务水平，而不是把仅仅为了财政目的而制定的简单粗糙的调查或控制指令，作为管理方法。

本文所阐述的构想，其基本着眼点是一种完整的，提供管理支持对策的可持续的因素，其主体目标仍然是经营实体，不管其性质如何，是公营的，私营的，还是公私合营的。

Appendix III   Key to Exercises

UNIT ONE
Reading Comprehension
I . 1. T   2. T   3. F   4. F   5. F   6. F   7. T   8. F   9. F   10. F
II . A (5)   B (10)   C (2)   D (9)   E (8)

Vocabulary
I . 1. be conserved   2. provides/has provided   3. dating   4. producing
   5. showed   6. has evolved   7. apply   8. was stored   9. be described
   10. settle
II . 1. B   2. B   3. A   4. D   5. C

UNIT TWO
Reading Comprehension
I . 1. T   2. T   3. F   4. F   5. T   6. T   7. F   8. F   9. T   10. T
II . A (5)   B (2)   C (1)   D (6)   E (4)

Vocabulary
I . 1. contains   2. enter   3. evaporated   4. ensure   5. condensed
   6. eliminates   7. be designated   8. was supported   9. being contaminated
   10. congregate
II . 1. C   2. C   3. B   4. A   5. B

UNIT THREE
Reading Comprehension
I . 1. T   2. T   3. F   4. T   5. F   6. T   7. T   8. T   9. F   10. F
II . A (7)   B (4)   C (6)   D (5)   E (3)

Vocabulary
I . 1. germinate   2. appreciate   3. be measured   4. has affected   5. commenced
   6. has been eradicated   7. has been assessed   8. outstrip   9. survive
   10. assumed
II . 1. D   2. A   3. D   4. B   5. A

UNIT FOUR

Reading Comprehension

I. 1. F 2. F 3. F 4. T 5. T 6. F 7. F 8. F 9. T 10. T

II. A (4) B (7) C (1) D (6) E (2)

Vocabulary

I. 1. created 2. be treated 3. suspended 4. dissolved 5. are being designed
 6. removes 7. mix 8. was promoted 9. organize 10. be sterilized

II. 1. B 2. D 3. C 4. A 5. C

UNIT FIVE

Reading Comprehension

I. 1. T 2. F 3. T 4. T 5. F 6. T 7. T 8. F 9. F 10. F

II. 1. D 2. B 3. C 4. A 5. C

Vocabulary

I. 1. detract 2. corrosive 3. deposits 4. ascertaining 5. clarified

II. 1. A 2. C 3. B 4. D 5. A

UNIT SIX

Reading Comprehension

I. 1. F 2. T 3. T 4. T 5. F 6. F 7. T 8. F 9. T 10. F

II. 1. D 2. B 3. A 4. C 5. B

Vocabulary

I. 1. travel 2. obtained 3. based on 4. to check 5. make up

II. 1. B 2. C 3. A 4. D 5. C

UNIT SEVEN

Reading Comprehension

I. 1. F 2. T 3. F 4. F 5. F 6. F 7. F 8. T 9. F 10. F

II. A (5) B (2) C (1) D (4) E (3)

Vocabulary

I. 1. circulating 2. maintain 3. utilized 4. protects 5. function 6. avoid
 7. includes 8. alter 9. combated 10. exist

II. 1. B 2. C 3. A 4. D 5. B

UNIT EIGHT
Reading Comprehension
I . 1. T 2. F 3. F 4. F 5. T 6. T 7. F 8. F 9. F 10. T
II . A (9) B (5) C (7) D (3) E (6)

Vocabulary
I . 1. demonstrated 2. synthesize 3. convert 4. involves 5. represent
6. requires 7. exemplified 8. proliferate 9. attacked 10. Specialized
II . 1. D 2. D 3. A 4. C 5. B

UNIT NINE
Reading Comprehension
I . 1. F 2. F 3. T 4. F 5. T 6. T 7. F 8. T 9. T 10. T
II . 1. B 2. C 3. A 4. A 5. C

Vocabulary
I . 1. hydraulic 2. irrigation 3. transmit 4. velocity 5. attraction
II . 1. B 2. A 3. C 4. C 5. A

UNIT TEN
Reading Comprehension
I . 1. T 2. F 3. F 4. T 5. F 6. T 7. F 8. F 9. T 10. F
II . A (7) B (2) C (6) D (1) E (4)

Vocabulary
I . 1. surrounded 2. retarded 3. achieved 4. sustain 5. control 6. relating
7. exposed 8. contrast 9. distinguish 10. remains
II . 1. A 2. C 3. D 4. B 5. A

UNIT ELEVEN
Reading Comprehension
I . 1. F 2. T 3. F 4. F 5. T 6. T 7. F 8. T 9. F 10. T
II . A (4) B (2) C (5) D (3) E (1)

Vocabulary
I . 1. reveals 2. dispose 3. constructed 4. diverted 5. collected 6. supply
7. carry off 8. recycling 9. extend 10. connected
II . 1. C 2. C 3. D 4. B 5. A

UNIT TWELVE
Reading Comprehension
I. 1. T   2. F   3. T   4. T   5. F   6. F   7. T   8. T   9. F   10. F
II. 1. A   2. B   3. D   4. C   5. C

Vocabulary
I. 1. organisms   2. species   3. occur   4. bacteria   5. depends on
II. 1. C   2. B   3. A   4. D   5. D

UNIT THIRTEEN
Reading Comprehension
I. 1. T   2. F   3. T   4. T   5. F   6. T   7. T   8. F   9. T   10. T
II. 1. C   2. A   3. B   4. C   5. A

Vocabulary
I. 1. adverse effects   2. accelerated   3. exist   4. electric power   5. factors
II. 1. B   2. A   3. D   4. C   5. D

UNIT FOURTEEN
Reading Comprehension
I. 1. T   2. F   3. F   4. T   5. F   6. F   7. F   8. F   9. T   10. T
II. 1. B   2. C   3. D   4. D   5. B

Vocabulary
I. 1. hazardous   2. potential   3. option   4. combustible   5. oxidation
II. 1. B   2. D   3. A   4. C   5. B

UNIT FIFTEEN
Reading Comprehension
I. 1. F   2. F   3. T   4. F   5. F   6. T   7. F   8. T   9. T   10. F
II. 1. C   2. B   3. B   4. D   5. B

Vocabulary
I. 1. feasibility   2. waste disposal   3. pollutants   4. dilution   5. detention
II. 1. B   2. B   3. D   4. C   5. D

UNIT SIXTEEN
Reading Comprehension

I. 1. F   2. T   3. F   4. T   5. F   6. F   7. F   8. T   9. F   10. T

II. 1. C   2. B   3. A   4. D   5. B

Vocabulary

I. 1. rather than   2. integrate... with   3. be correspondent to   4. characteristic of
    5. connect... with

II. 1. C   2. D   3. A   4. B   5. C

图书在版编目（CIP）数据

建筑类专业英语. 给水排水与环境保护. 第1册/朱满才，王学玲主编. —北京：中国建筑工业出版社，1997（2005重印）
高等学校试用教材
ISBN 978-7-112-03032-3

Ⅰ. 建… Ⅱ. ①朱…②王… Ⅲ. ①建筑学-英语-高等学校-教材②给水-英语-高等学校-教材③排水-英语-高等学校-教材④环境保护-英语-高等学校-教材　Ⅳ. H31

中国版本图书馆CIP数据核字（2005）第090440号

本书是按国家教委颁布的《大学英语专业阅读阶段教学基本要求》规定编写的专业英语教材。本册包括给水历史、水的净化、环境工程、水与大气污染及水力学等方面内容。全书分16个单元，每单元除正课文外，还有两篇阅读材料，均配有必要的注释。正课文还配有词汇表和练习，书后附有总词汇表、参考译文和练习答案。供高等学校本专业学生三年级上学期使用，也可供有关人员自学。

高等学校试用教材
建筑类专业英语
给水排水与环境保护
第一册
朱满才　王学玲　主编
胡继兰　孙晓梅
徐飞珍　吴晓光　　编
项宏萍　　　　　主审

*

中国建筑工业出版社出版、发行（北京西郊百万庄）
各地新华书店、建筑书店经销
廊坊市海涛印刷有限公司印刷

*

开本：787×1092毫米　1/16　印张：11　字数：267千字
1997年6月第一版　2017年1月第十五次印刷
定价：**20.00元**
ISBN 978-7-112-03032-3
（20897）

版权所有　翻印必究
如有印装质量问题，可寄本社退换
（邮政编码 100037）